ON MY WAY TO NOLLYWOOD

NOLLYWOOD

Dr Boniface Ikejiani

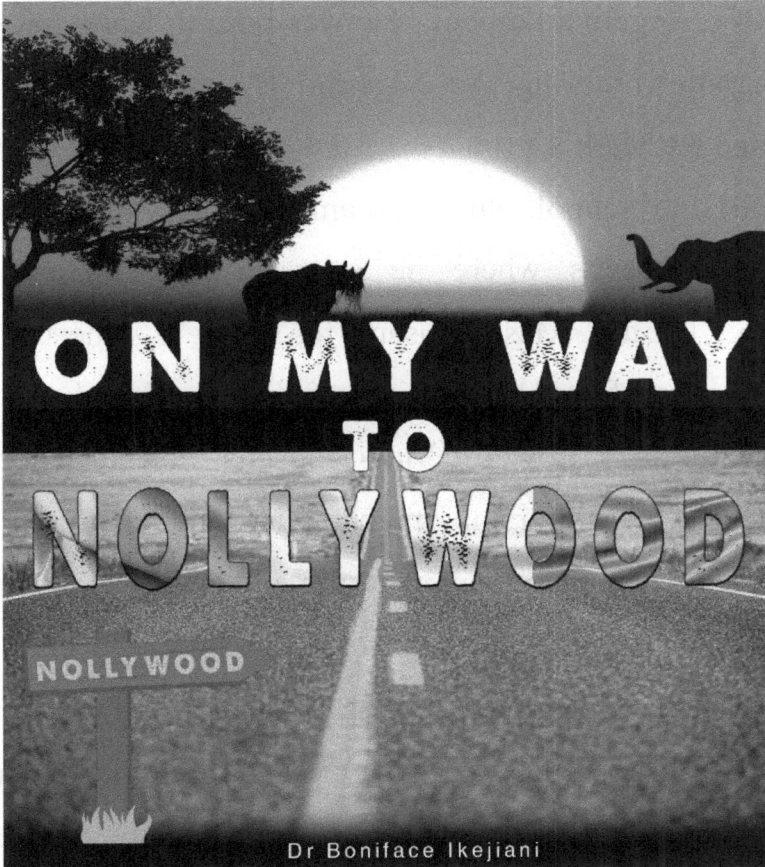

Author Dr Boniface Ikejiani

About the Author

Dr. Boniface Ikejiani is the sixth child of Late Mr. Boniface and Mrs. Angelina Ikejiani. He was born in Kano but grew up in Nnewi during the Nigerian Biafran civil war. He attended St Mark's primary school after which he attended Nnewi High School, Nnewi Anambra State. He proceeded to Massachusetts where he attended Bay State Junior College, Boston, Massachusetts for about a semester after which he transferred to and graduated from the University of Massachusetts, Lowell Massachusetts as a chemical engineer with minors in mathematics and chemistry. He worked for several years as a health and beauty aids product developer. He proceeded to medical school and graduated from Indiana University School of medicine, Indianapolis, Indiana. He completed a one year preliminary general surgery residency at Wright State University School of medicine, Dayton Ohio. Dr. Boniface Ikejiani completed his residency in obstetrics and gynecology at Northeastern Ohio University School of medicine, Canton Ohio. His work has taken him across many nations to include Nigeria, USA,

Author Dr Boniface Ikejiani

Canada, Jamaica, Venezuela and many others. He has travelled to more than five hundred cities around the world and has extensive experience about Nigeria, USA, Canada, England, Netherland, France, Germany, Belgium, Italy, China, Ethiopia, Kenya, Uganda, Senegal, Ghana, Togo, and several other countries. His hobbies include reading, travelling and always seeking solutions everywhere. He has visited many centers of excellence in arts in several parts of the world. He is blessed with four wonderful children; Dara, Anna, David, and Joshua. The drive for excellence in the area of Nollywood movie encouraged him to write this book, "On my way to Nollywood" to bring needed information to new entrants to Nollywood.

The author can be reached via email at:bikejiani99@gmail.com

Author Dr Boniface Ikejiani

Preface

The purpose of this book is to bring the much needed light to Nollywood among the new entrants and open the eyes of veteran practitioners in every aspect of Nollywood.

The chapters are ordered in such a way to emphasize the contribution of every department in the development of Nollywood.

I had tremendous communication with friends and associates all over the globe in the process of developing this book. I spoke with many producers, directors, actors, actresses, script writers, continuity experts, caterers, cameramen, and editors. My sincere gratitude goes to Mr. Joe Aihende who was very insightful and introduced me to some talented scriptwriters. My sincere thank you to Dr. Uchenna Nwabufo Akpom who was very gracious in reading every piece of this writing from the outlines to chapter formation, book cover design and gave some interesting suggestions. My gratitude goes to Mr. Azubueze Ikejiani who was instrumental as a bouncing platform for all the ideas in this book while in the early stage of conception. My deep gratitude goes to Prof. Dr. Prosper Igboeli who is a colleague, friend, mentor, and coach for his love of diligence, knowledge, and excellence.

I owe a big thank you to my entire household who participated directly and indirectly in the development of this book. My special thank you to my children, Ms. Dara Ikejiani, Ms. Anna Ikejiani, David Ikejiani and Joshua Ikejiani for all their sacrifices in the course of writing this book.

My thank you go to all the editors who worked really diligently in the review of all the work in order to bring excellence to Nollywood. A special thank you goes to Ms. Uche Ajukwu, Chrisfrank Chizobam, Mrs. Otonsimake Brown and Ms. Adora Ajuzie who critiqued the various cover designs for this book.

My ultimate interest is that this book will open up new doors, bring out the best and foster excellence in all the new entrants in Nollywood, Africa and beyond.

Author Dr Boniface Ikejiani

On my way to Nollywood
By

[DR BONIFACE IKEJIANI]

Text Copyright © [DR BONIFACE IKEJIANI]

Legal & Disclaimer

Author Dr Boniface Ikejiani

costs, and expenses, including any legal fees potentially resulting from the application of any of the information provided by this book. This disclaimer applies to any loss, damages or injury caused by the use and application, whether directly or indirectly, of any advice or information presented, whether for breach of contract, tort, negligence, personal injury, criminal intent, or under any other cause of action.

You agree to accept all risks of using the information presented in this book.

You agree that by continuing to read this book, where appropriate and/or necessary, you shall consult a professional (including but not limited to your doctor, attorney, or financial advisor or such other advisor as needed) before using any of the suggested remedies, techniques, or information in this book.

Author Dr Boniface Ikejiani

Table of Contents

Chapter 1
Acting

- What is acting?   27
- Types of acting   28
- Importance of acting   28
- Acting tips   30

Chapter 2
Script writing

- What is script writing?   32
- History of script writing.   33
- What makes a good script writer?   33
- How to become a script writer?   34

Chapter 3
Continuity writing

- What is continuity writing?   35
- Types of continuity writing in filmmaking.   35
- Importance of continuity writing in filmmaking.   36
- What makes a good continuity writer?   36

Author Dr Boniface Ikejiani

Chapter 4
Script Editing/Proof Reading

- What is script editing/proofreading?   37
- Why are scripts edited and proofread?   38
- Script editor software.   38
- Importance of script editing/proofreading.   38

Chapter 5
Directing

- What is film directing?   39
- The qualities of a good director?   40
- The functions of a director.   41
- Importance of directing in the movie industry.   41

Chapter 6
Stunting/Special Talent

- Types Of Talent   45
- Film Set Etiquette   51

Chapter 7
Camera operation

- Digital Compression System   56
- Lens Optics and elements of photography   57
- Understanding the concept of exposure lattitude   63
- Film laboratory and film telecine   64
- The use of color temperature in photography   65
- Measuring light intensity   68
- The principles of electricity   70
- Television camera operations   72
- Television camera controls   77
- Television camera movement   77
- Career opportunities   83

Chapter 8
Lightning

- Lighting equipment and lamps   86
- Lighting for scenery   89
- Lighting for projections   90

Author Dr Boniface Ikejiani

Chapter 9

Production designing

- What is production design? 93
- Impact of production design on production. 96

Chapter 10

Sound Recording

- Microphones 98
- Microphone polar patterns 99
- Microphone techniques used in studio recording 102
- How to choose the right microphones 104
- How will a room's design affect the sound and feel of a recording? 106

Chapter 11

Music/Sound tract production

- What is music/sound tract production? 107
- The importance of music/sound tract production. 107
- Music/sound tract production software programs. 108
- Music/sound tract equipment. 108

Chapter 12

Still Photography

- Camera modes and uses   111
- ISO settings in Digital Photography   118
- Focusing options   119
- Valuable composition tips   121
- Night photography   123
- Intro to lighting   124
- Drive modes   125
- White balance   127
- Adjusting white balance   128
- Adjusting white balance manually   130
- Exposure compensation   131
- Application of basic elements of composition   133

Chapter 13

Video editing

- Why video editing is needed in the movie industry?
  134
- Best video editing software programs.   135

Author Dr Boniface Ikejiani

Chapter 14

Sound Recording

- History of sound recording.   136
- Sound recording software.   137
- Sound recording equipment.   137
- Sound recording app.   137

Chapter 15

Subtitling

- Why are movies subtitled?   139
- Subtitling rules.   140
- Subtitling apps.   140
- Best subtitling companies.   140

Chapter 16

Lip Synchronization

- What is lip synchronization?   141
- The importance of lip synchronization in movies.142

Chapter 17

Voice over/Voice talent

- Who is a voice over?   143
- Voice over jobs.   143
- Best voice over software.   144
- Why is voice over needed?   144

Chapter 18

Speech doctoring

- What is speech doctoring?   145
- How is speech doctored?   146
- Top best speech doctoring software.   146

Chapter 19

Choreography/Dance Instructing/Dancing

- What is choreography?   147
- Who is dance instructing?   147
- What is choreography important in filmmaking? 148
- What is the importance of dance instructing?   148

Chapter 20

Special Effect

- What is special effect?   149
- How is special effect done?   149
- Best software for special effect.   150
- Importance of special effects in filmmaking.   150

Chapter 21

Animation Production

- How is animation produced?   151
- Importance of animation production.   152
- Best animation software.   153

Chapter 22

Costuming/Tailoring

- What is costuming?   154
- Functions of a good costumier.   154
- Qualifications of a good costumier.   155
- Importance of costuming/tailoring.   155

Author Dr Boniface Ikejiani

Chapter 23

Make-up/Hair artist

- Who is a make-up/hair artist?   156
- What are their functions?   156
- What are their qualifications?   157
- Qualities of a good make-up/hair artist.   157

Chapter 24

Line Producing

- What is line producing?   159
- How to become a line producer.   160
- Qualities of a good line producer.   160

Chapter 25

Catering Services

- A brief history of catering   163
- Kitchen tools and equipment   165
- Development of food service   170
- New trends in food service   172
- Skills needed in catering service   174
- Types of catering services   176

Author Dr Boniface Ikejiani

- Laws, Regulations, and Licenses for Catering Services in Nigeria   180
- Dos and Don'ts of catering service   181
- Consumer goodwill and food service ethics   184
- The seven rules of catering service   185

Chapter 26

Property management

- What is property management?   188
- Why is property management needed in Hollywood?   189
- What makes a good property manager?   189

Chapter 27

Production management

- What is production management?   190
- What are the functions of a production manager? 191
- Scope of production management.   191
- Qualities of a good production manager.   191

Author Dr Boniface Ikejiani

Chapter 28

Production designing

- What is production designing? 193

- How to become a production designer. 193

- The importance of production designing in filmmaking. 194

- What makes a good production designer? 194

Chapter 29

Movie Funding

- How are movies fund? 195

- How to get funding for your movie. 196

Chapter 30

Equipment Leasing/Studio service provider

- How are equipment leased? 197

- The best studio service providers in Hollywood. 198

Author Dr Boniface Ikejiani

Chapter 31

Video Rentals

- Top video rentals.   199
- Impact of video renting on Hollywood.   200

Chapter 32

Marketing/Distribution

- Importance of marketing and distributing movies. 201
- Best marketing/distributing strategies.   201
- Best marketing/distributing companies in Hollywood.

                                                       202

Chapter 33

Exhibition

- What is movie exhibition?   203
- Types of exhibition.   204
- Importance of exhibition.   204

Chapter 34

Painting Sculptures

- The roles of art in the movies.   205
- Artwork used in movies.   206

Chapter 35

Printing Posters and Jackets

- How to print posters and jackets.   236
- The cost of printing posters and jackets for movies.

                                                      237
- Best posters and jackets printing companies.   237

Chapter 36

DVD/VCD Replication

- How are DVDs/VCDs replicated?   238
- The cost of replication.   239
- Best DVD replication services.   239

Author Dr Boniface Ikejiani

Chapter 37

Movie Reporting

- What is movie reporting?   240
- How are movies reported?   241
- Importance of movie reporting.   241

Chapter 38

Training/Capacity Building

- What is capacity building?   242
- The roles of training/capacity building in Hollywood.   243

Chapter 39

Set Construction

- What is set construction?   244
- Set construction techniques.   244
- Functions of set construction.   245

Chapter 40

Poster Pasting

- Why are posters pasted? 246
- Importance of poster pasting to the movie industry. 247

Chapter 41

Carpentry

- Why is carpentry needed in filmmaking? 250
- The key skills of a carpenter. 250

Chapter 42

Story Sales

- What is story sales? 252
- How to make the best story sales? 253
- The attributes of a compelling sales story. 253

Chapter 43

Poster Pasting

- Why are posters pasted?   254

- Importance of poster pasting to the movie industry.

     255

Chapter 44

Artiste Management

- Who is an artiste manager?   256

- How are artistes managed?   257

- Qualities of a competent artiste manager.   257

Chapter 45

Promotion

- How are movies promoted?   258

- Importance of movie promotion.   259

- Best promotion techniques.   259

- Best promotion companies.   260

Author Dr Boniface Ikejiani

Chapter 46

Insurance Cover for Artiste

- How are artistes insured?   261
- The importance of providing insurance cover for artistes.   262
- Best insurance companies for artistes.   263

Chapter 47
Book Publishing

- How are books published?   264
- The cost of publishing a book.   265
- Best publishing companies.   265

Chapter 48

Equipment Manufacture

- What equipment is needed in Nollywood?   266
- The best equipment manufacturing companies in Hollywood.   267

Chapter 49

Contract Agreement writing

- How to write contract agreement in Nollywood. 269
- Tips for writing the best contract agreement. 270
- The importance of writing contract agreement. 270

Chapter 50
Business of Nollywood

References

Introduction

Nollywood is the official name of the Nigerian film industry. The name is carved from Hollywood, the official name of the American film industry. By combining the two words, "Hollywood" and "Nigeria," this name was coined for Africa's largest film industry and the second largest in the world, after Bollywood, the Indian movie industry.

The journey of Nollywood started long ago with the likes of Hubert Ogunde, Baba Sala, Ade Love, and other movie giants who entertained their audience with rib-cracking and wisdom-filled movies. However, the movie industry was still relatively unknown and was not identified by a special name.

Author Dr Boniface Ikejiani

This all changed in 1992 when Kenneth Nnebue produced the first movie on video. When this electronics salesman produced *Living in Bondage* in 1992, hardly did he know that he had laid the foundation stone of a multi-billion dollar industry. The movie sold over a million copies without any form of electronic advertisement. Rather, the promotion was done by using the local advertising technique – via street vendors. As the saying goes, "the rest is history." Nollywood was born.

A study conducted in 2009 showed that Nollywood had leapfrogged Hollywood to become the world's second largest movie industry after the famous India's Bollywood. Some years later, in 2014, data released by the Nigerian government showed the economic value of the Nigerian movie industry.

According to the data, 1,844 movies were produced in the preceding year, 2013, while the movie sector was said to be worth $3.3 billion. The sector covers movies made in English, Hausa, Yoruba, Igbo, Edo, Urhobo, Itsekiri, Efik, and any other language from the over 300 languages spoken in Nigeria, Africa's largest country.

It is true that Nollywood has come of age. It has really matured and has gained international recognition. However, only a few people have an idea of what contributes to the success of the industry. The question then is, "What makes up the Nollywood?"

In this book, I will go into a0 comprehensive explanation of the different professionals and others who are behind the success of the industry over the years.

So, if you are a Nollywood enthusiast or a stakeholder in the Nigerian movie industry, sit back and enjoy as I take you through this journey on the exegesis on various professionals behind the success of Africa's largest movie industry.

Author Dr Boniface Ikejiani

Chapter 1
Acting

- What is acting?

Acting is an activity in which a story is told by means of its enactment by an actor or actress who adopts a character - in theatre, television, film, radio, or any other medium that makes use of the mimetic mode.

Acting involves a broad range of skills, including a well-developed imagination, emotional facility, physical expressivity, vocal projection, clarity of speech, and the

Author Dr Boniface Ikejiani

ability to interpret drama. Acting also demands an ability to employ dialects, accents, improvisation, observation and emulation, mime, and stage combat. Many actors train at length in specialist programmes or colleges to develop these skills. The vast majority of professional actors have undergone extensive training. Actors and actresses will often have many instructors and teachers for a full range of training involving singing, scene-work, audition techniques, and acting for camera.

- Types of acting

There are two major types of acting – theatre and television/film. The three of the major differences between those two types of acting are:
1. The audience location.
2. The material.
3. The iconic nature of the characters.

- Importance of acting

Acting has many benefits:

1. Socialization – theater courses allow interaction with different personalities, so you will have the opportunity to improve your communication skills;

2. Enriches vocabulary – through the roles that are being performed, you can learn lots of words (neologisms but also archaisms or regionalisms, depending on the play), enriching your vocabulary;

3. Body expressiveness – following the acting classes, you can learn how to control your movements and gestures;

4. Verbal expressiveness – all actors know the importance of intonation, tone or speed of the words spoken. You can learn to correctly transmit a message and to interpret correctly what others say;

5. Ability to speak in public – playing a role in front of an audience can help develop the ability to keep perceptions or speeches in front of other people;

6. General culture – by getting in touch with plays, you can learn a lot about both the authors of the plays and the social or historical context they refer to, thus improving general culture;

7. Self-confidence – the long-term consequence of theater courses refers to the stimulation of self-confidence. A successful interpretation on the stage, public applause are among the elements that will boost your self-confidence;

Author Dr Boniface Ikejiani

8. Learning abilities – although it does not seem like a great intellectual effort, interpreting a role puts lots of processes in motion, improving them;

9. Self-knowledge – although it may seem paradoxical, pretending to be someone else, entering a character's "skin", can present you a perfect opportunity to learn a lot about yourself. Discovering personality traits that match the interpreted characters or totally opposed characters, you can begin understanding in depth what the character means, which are his moral values and how emotions influence people's actions.

10. Auto-control – theater classes teach how to master your emotions, how to channel them in a positive way and how to build appropriate responses to different situations. By exercising the ability to overcome the trackage on the stage, you can learn that you are the "master" of your own emotions. This will positively influence relationships with others.

- Acting tips

1. "Find the joy" – Jonathan Groff
2. "Study, study, study" – Keith David
3. "Don't worry about what the casting director is thinking" – Michaela Watkins

Author Dr Boniface Ikejiani

4. "Risk failure to make truthful discoveries" – Lupita Nyong'o

5. "Believe in your goals" – James Wolk

6. "Treat auditions like rehearsals" – Amy Schumer

7. "Follow what you love" – Derek Hough

8. "Pay attention to what you know" – Patrick Stewart

9. "Go ahead and produce your own work" – Kevin Spacey

10. "Make the role yours" – Timothy Simons

11. "Lighten up and have fun" – Alan Cumming

12. "Share your inner uniqueness" – Joshua Henry

13. "Avoid desperation" – Michael Emerson

14. "Push yourself beyond what you think you know" – Vanessa Shaw

15. "Don't just dream" – Charlotte Kate Fox

16. "Don't try to be someone else" – Laura Benanti

17. "Explore the world outside acting" – Celia Keenan-Bolger

18. "It's ok to get a little lost" – Michael Esper

19. "Create characters from the outside in" – Mark Ruffalo

20. "Write your own parts" – Ricky Gervais

Author Dr Boniface Ikejiani

Chapter 2
Script writing

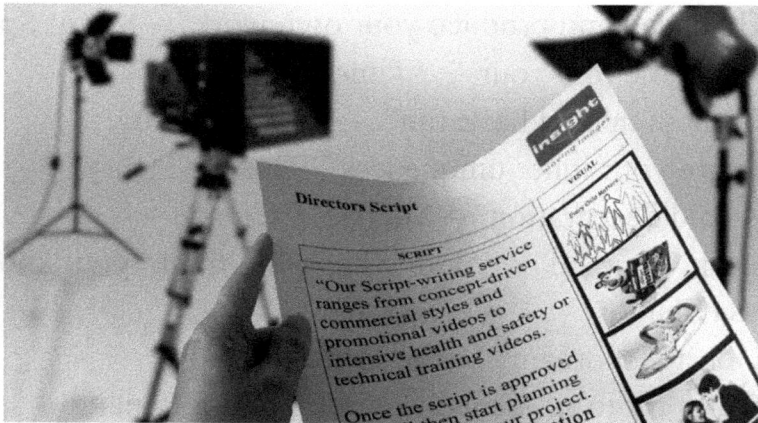

- What is script writing?

Script writing (screenwriting) is the art and craft of writing scripts for mass media such as feature films, television productions or video games. It is the main part of any episode interactive story. It influences how the characters can act, talk, and generally, how the story moves or flows. It is frequently a freelance profession.

Author Dr Boniface Ikejiani

- History of script writing.

The true first scenario is considered to be from George Melies' 1902 film – "The Journey to the moon". The movie is silent, but the script still contains descriptions and action lines that resemble a modern script. With the passing of time and the movies starting to be longer and more complex, the script has become more prominent in the industry. The introduction of cinemas also affected the development of scenarios as audiences became more widespread and more sophisticated, so stories needed to be just as good.

Once the first non-silent movie was released in 1927, the script has become an extremely important position in Hollywood. The studio system of the 1930s has only increased its importance, as studio managers have created productivity. Around 1970 was created the first "spec" scenario and a change of industry for writers.

- What makes a good script writer?

Scriptwriters are responsible for researching the story, developing the narrative, writing the screenplay, and delivering it, in the required format, to development executives. Screenwriters, therefore, have great influence over the creative direction and emotional impact of the screenplay and, arguably, of the finished film. Screenwriters either pitch original ideas to producers, in the hope that they will be optioned or sold, or are commissioned by a producer

Author Dr Boniface Ikejiani

to create a screenplay from a concept, true story, existing screen work or literary work, such as a novel, poem, play, comic book or short story.

A good script writer is driven by passion, reading, writing and rewriting. A good script writer trusts their instincts and the power of their imagination and creativity. A good script writer should spend as much time reading other scripts as they spend writing them. Reading scripts is essential in learning the basics of what to and what not to do when writing your own.

* How to become a script writer?

Becoming a scriptwriter requires a lot of motivation. If you love writing for the sake of writing, that's the first and the most important step in becoming a scriptwriter.

To become a successful script writer, you need to have a driving reason to write, to trust your instincts and write what excites you, to not let the marketplace rule your imagination, to aim to some writing goals, to evoke emotions and feelings in the reader.

Chapter 3
Continuity writing

- What is continuity writing?

Continuity writing is a job done by writers that have to maintain the storyline of the series and make sure it is following a continuous story. It deals with the consistency of the characteristics of people, plot, objects, and places seen by the viewer over some period of time. It is relevant in filmmaking and contributes to the overall success of the movie production.

- Types of continuity writing in filmmaking.

1. Continuity of Information.
2. Continuity of Action.
3. Continuity of Looks.

Author Dr Boniface Ikejiani

4. Continuity of Movements.
5. Conventional Continuity.

- Importance of continuity writing in filmmaking.

Continuity is very important. It is one of the areas that the emerging film maker consistently overlooks with negative consequences.
Continuity is important because as long as it evolves, it has to stick to the original story.

- What makes a good continuity writer?

A good continuity writer should be detail oriented so as to pay attention to all the little details, reliable because he may always be counted on to do a good job and ready for a challenge so that he would jump into the new project with an initiative.

Author Dr Boniface Ikejiani

Chapter 4
Script Editing/Proof Reading

- What is script editing/proofreading?

Script editing or proofreading is the reading of a gallery proof or an electronic copy of a publication to detect and correct production errors of text or art.

Author Dr Boniface Ikejiani

- Why are scripts edited and proofread?

Scripts are usually edited and proofread to be sure that it has no errors and to see that every sentence makes sense and that the text is readable. Usually, when you proofread, you can also make some text changes.

- Script editor software

1. Celtx
2. Highland
3. Fade In

- Importance of script editing/proofreading.

One of the first steps for creating a video project is the script writing. A script is necessary whether a video project is a feature-length motion picture, a short training video or even an account of a family vacation. A script is a document that describes the video, which includes descriptions of the various shots and any dialogue/voiceovers.

A script also serves as a planning device for the video. It describes the stock footage that is used, which locations where certain scenes will be shot, what occurs in each shot, and what is included in each shot.

Author Dr Boniface Ikejiani

Chapter 5
Directing

- What is Film Directing?

Film directing involves controlling the artistic and dramatic aspects, visualizing the screenplay or script and guiding the technical crew and actors in the fulfilment of that vision.

The film's director primary task is to interpret the screenplay and translate it visually. He is the creative mind that chooses the aesthetical and technical specifications to be implemented in his vision. From the early stages through to the end, the director is actively involved. Directing movies requires extensive command of the craft. It takes years of

Author Dr Boniface Ikejiani

dedication and hard work to master, and when art becomes part and parcel of the artist, it takes a century or never to forget.

• The qualities of a good director?

During a film production, the director assumes very many roles. He exhibits different qualities and traits, be aware and as well understands the cultural and political issues that surround his movie asides mastering the production process and storytelling techniques. The bigger the qualities of a good director the better will the film be. The following qualities make a good director:

1.   A strong sense of authority for leading the team;
2.   Excellent communication skills to articulate what their production goals are;
3.   Very creative to be able to generate ideas for stories, backgrounds, music, etc.;
4.   Decisiveness to make decisions and stick to them;
5.   Sense of drive and ambition;
6.   Ability to handle pressure well;
7.   Open minded;
8.   Problem solving so that they would be able to identify problems and figure out a way to fix them;
9.   Technologically Savvy;
10.   Visionary.

Author Dr Boniface Ikejiani

- The functions of a director.

The director is responsible for the artistic side of the film. Everything that will appear on the screen is the result of the director's vision of the script.

1. He collaborates with the producer to determine the distribution of the film;

2. He participates along with the production manager at the location of the shooting locations;

3. He approves scenario extracts made by the production manager;

4. He establishes together with the image director the necessary details of the technical equipment for shooting;

5. He approves designs for decorations and arrangements;

6. He establishes together with the sound engineer of the film the sound recording solutions in critical locations;

7. During the filming, he collaborates with the actors to understand the roles they have to play;

8. He chooses the doubles of the cadres who will enter the post-production stage and together with the sound editor, he sets the final soundtrack of the film;

9. He assists in mixing the sound components of the film.

- Importance of directing in the movie industry.

The importance of directing in the movie industry is given by all the details a director needs to stay focused on and pay attention to. Directing a movie is the creative translation of

Author Dr Boniface Ikejiani

the written scenario of the movie into real-life images and sounds on the screen. A director has a lot of responsibilities, and practically, the whole movie depends on him. Everything revolves around the director and the production schedule. They must oversee the several stages of production including principal photography. Rewriting of the script, rehearsals, lighting, costumes, décor, props, camera, actors are all supervised by the director, who's often multitasking and micromanaging.

Author Dr Boniface Ikejiani

Chapter 6
Stunting/Special Talent

Stunt performing in the movie industry involves the performance of some risky acts during a movie. Most times, this may involve martial arts, car racing, rock climbing, and what have you.

The goal of performing stunts in movies is to increase the action-level of the movies. These stunts are usually considered some of the highlights of a movie and are expected to serve different purposes, ranging from entertainment to increase in the acceptance and value of the movies where stunts are performed.

Author Dr Boniface Ikejiani

In some cases, stunt performers are hired to serve as a perfect replacement for an actor when stunting in needed. The hired stunt performer, otherwise known as double, will fill in for the main actor to perform the different tricks.

It is important that a double has some specialized skills that qualify him for the role of a stuntman.

Types of Talents

For a stuntman, some special talents, apart from acting, are expected to be able to qualify for the role. These special talents are divided into five sections. The sections, named Group A to Group G are:

Author Dr Boniface Ikejiani

Group A

Fighting: The stuntman should be either an experienced boxer or martial arts expert or both combined. These skills are required in areas where a physical fighting is actually needed.

Group B

Falling: This stunt role is for stuntmen that are experienced in high diving, tramp lining, and other related acts.

Group C

Riding and driving: In this category, the ability to ride horses, drive cars, and ride motorcycles are the basic requirements from a would-be stuntman. This is especially true in movies where car racing, horse racing, or bike racing is an integral part of the movie.

Author Dr Boniface Ikejiani

Group D

Agility and strength: This is a test of an actor's gymnastics skills. This may include rock climbing, powerlifting, and the likes.

Author Dr Boniface Ikejiani

Group E

Water: You must be a good swimmer to be considered for this role.

Generally, it is required that you have qualifications in a minimum of four groups while you are trained in a minimum of three categories under a group.

For instance, if you are in Group C, you must be trained to handle the categories in that group in addition to having expertise in three other groups.

In each qualification, you must have a minimum of one year experience too. It is imperative that you keep updating your qualifications and skills from time to time to meet the job demands and the challenges of stunting.

Author Dr Boniface Ikejiani

Film set etiquette

How you conduct yourself while on a film set is a sign of professionalism you should cultivate as a professional. Knowing how to conduct yourself is a good way to contribute meaningfully to the industry. It goes a long way in shaping your career and making you a force to be reckoned with within the movie industry.

Some important film set etiquettes you should understand and practice are:

Rule 1: Mind your manners

When on the set, it is important that you watch how you relate with other crew members, giving unsolicited advice, or putting on an attitude that doesn't portray you as a professional.

Rule 2: Actors should always stay in the front of the camera always

This is a preventive measure against an actor stopping himself or herself while in the middle of a take. An actor is forbidden from judging his personal performance or second-guessing the director. If you are an actor, you may have no idea of what the Director's plan is. Going beyond your boundary may mess up an important take.

Rule 3: It is the exclusive right of the director to say "Cut"

Theoretically speaking, it is only the Director that is empowered to use that word. There are some exceptions, though. For instance, the First Assistant Director who also doubles as the primary safety officer may yell cut if he notices something that is out of place. The Stunt Coordinator can also pronounce the word if he sees something inimical to the stunt. However, other crew members are forbidden from taking that role.

Rule 4: Reserve your comment until the end of the take

While on set, you all have the freedom of speech to express your mind over something out of place. However, it is unprofessional to interrupt a take with your complaint. You must wait until the end of a take before you make your mind known to the construction crew.

Rule 5: Learn the rules of your set

Each of the sets on a movie set is unique. Some sets are lively where everyone is free to fool around without having any negative impact on the set. Some sets require that you are cool and quiet. This may be a prerequisite for the actors to work to the best of their abilities. So, you must endeavor to know what the rules are in your set and abide by them.

Rule 6: Avoid wearing bright clothes

Wearing bright shirt on a set will obviously enhance your beauty. However, it can also have a negative effect when lighting a scene. Therefore, you should learn to avoid wearing some bright colors such as yellow, white, and light grays. These are the colors that can unwittingly bounce more light on the scene.

Author Dr Boniface Ikejiani

Chapter 7
Camera Operation

The camera operation encompasses all the activities that are carried out using the camera. The activities here involve television production and camera and lighting techniques. This is one of the core areas of film production.

Author Dr Boniface Ikejiani

Some of the area covered by camera operation includes:

1. Principle of color television production

Color television refers to the transmission technology used in television production that includes a treatise of the color of the picture so that a movie will be displayed on the television screen in color including white and black.

This is in sharp contrast to the previous television technology where pictures were shown in black and white or monochrome. There has been a gradual shift in color from the monochromatic color scheme to the color television technology that makes showing pictures in their real colors possible.

The principle behind color production is very simple and interesting. In the monochrome color, the image is usually displayed in grey scale or shades of grey. Color production is an improvement on this grayscale production. In color production, a color image is produced when three monochrome images are broadcasted. One of the monochrome images will be produced in red color while the others will be produced in green and blue respectively in conformity to the RGB principle.

When these three monochrome images are displayed in quick succession, the result is seen by the viewer as a full-color image that is produced through the blending of the monochrome images.

Digital compression system

The digital compression system refers to a system that is used to set multiple programs in the Mbps stream. This compression system is exclusively limited to digital TV.

For an image to be compressed for transmission, the broadcasters will make use of the MPEG-2 (Moving Picture Experts Group-2) compression system. This system allows the broadcaster to specify the bit rate and screen size they want to use when encoding the image. The broadcasters have tons of bit rates to choose from according to what they intend to broadcast.

Author Dr Boniface Ikejiani

The introduction of digital compression system has revolutionized the Broadcasting industry in recent years as different techniques have been developed to make color broadcasting possible. With the standardization of the algorithm used for the compression, there has been a rapid improvement in the industry. The standardization has also led to a reduction in the bandwidth required to broadcast high-quality TV signals by broadcasters.

Principle of digital camera systems

A digital camera is a type of camera that is used for producing images that are storable in digital memory and can be printed or displayed on a projector or screen.

Author Dr Boniface Ikejiani

Most of the cameras in the world today are digital. They are used effectively in many devices such as mobile phones and PDAs (Personal Digital Assistants). Digital cameras use an optical system that involves focusing on light with a lens that has a variable diaphragm when it is used on a device that has the ability to capture images.

The shutter and diaphragm of the camera will admit the right amount of light to the image-picking device which is an electronic device. Unlike chemical or film cameras, digital cameras are designed with the ability to instantly display images on any screen as soon as the image is recorded. It can also store such images or delete them from its memory.

A larger percentage of these cameras can record moving objects along with the sound. Some of them are even equipped with image-editing abilities to make the work of the cameraman easy.

Digital cameras come in four different types according to their sensor technology. These four technologies include:

- CCD (Charged Coupled Device)

- EMCCD (Electron Multiplying Charge Coupled Device)

- CMOS (Complementary metal-oxide semiconductor)

Author Dr Boniface Ikejiani

- ICCD (Impactron Charged Coupled Device)

However, the two major types are CMOS and CCD.

The CCD ranks among the oldest technologies used for image capture in digital cameras. Over the years, it has proved to be a reliable sensor for a high-quality image. The sensor comes with a single amplifier that can be used for a wide range of pixels. It offers more noise control and dynamic range than the CMOS sensor. It also requires more power than the CMOS.

On the other hand, the CMOS sensor has an amplifier for each sensor and consumes less power than the CCD sensor. It has gradually been upgraded to surpass the CCD in all areas which have led to a more efficient and better-performing camera sensor.

In general, the overall performance or quality of a camera is independent of the sensor type but its image processing ability.

Lens optics and elements of photography

A lens is an optical device used for transmission purpose. An optical lens uses refraction to disperse or focus on a beam of light. A simple optical lens consists primarily of a transparent material for its performance. On the other hand,

Author Dr Boniface Ikejiani

a compound lens is a combination of a good number of simple lenses that are arranged on a single axis.

Some of the important elements of photography are:

• **Hyperfocal distance.**

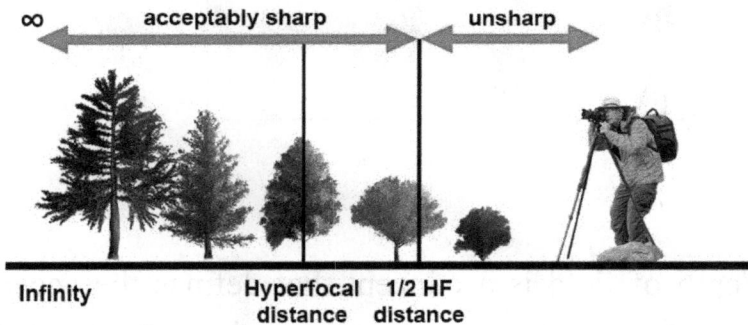

Hyperfocal distance is a measure of the distance between the closest object to a camera lens that can be seen when the lens is focused at infinity. Since it is the focus distance under the ideal depth of field, it is the best distance you should focus when using a fixed-focus camera. Nevertheless, the hyperfocal distance is a function of the degree of sharpness that is considered acceptable. In this case, what is acceptable is specified in the diameter limit of the circle of confusion and is the size diameter that a small point can spread out on either the film or digital sensor or any other imaging medium.

- **Depth of field.**

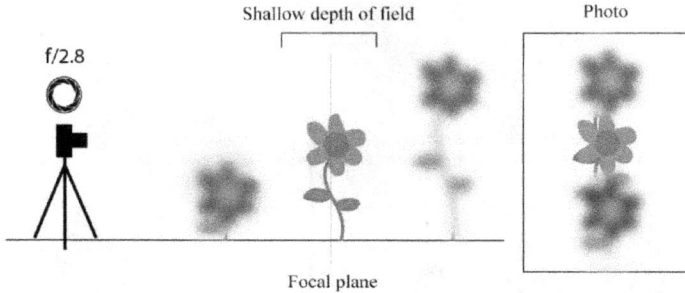

The depth of field is a concept that defines the acceptable range of distance that an image may be considered sharp. This is determined by some factors such as aperture, camera type, viewing distance, focusing distance, and print size. The depth makes its transition from sharpness to bluntness a gradual process so that any item in the back or the front of the focusing distance successively loses its sharpness.

Therefore, within the depth of field, the dullness of an image cannot be perceived when viewed under a normal condition. In some cases, it may be ideal that the whole image is sharp and that will require a large depth of field. On the other hand, you may only need a small depth of field. This will require focusing on the main object while the background and foreground are de-emphasized.

- **Angle of view.**

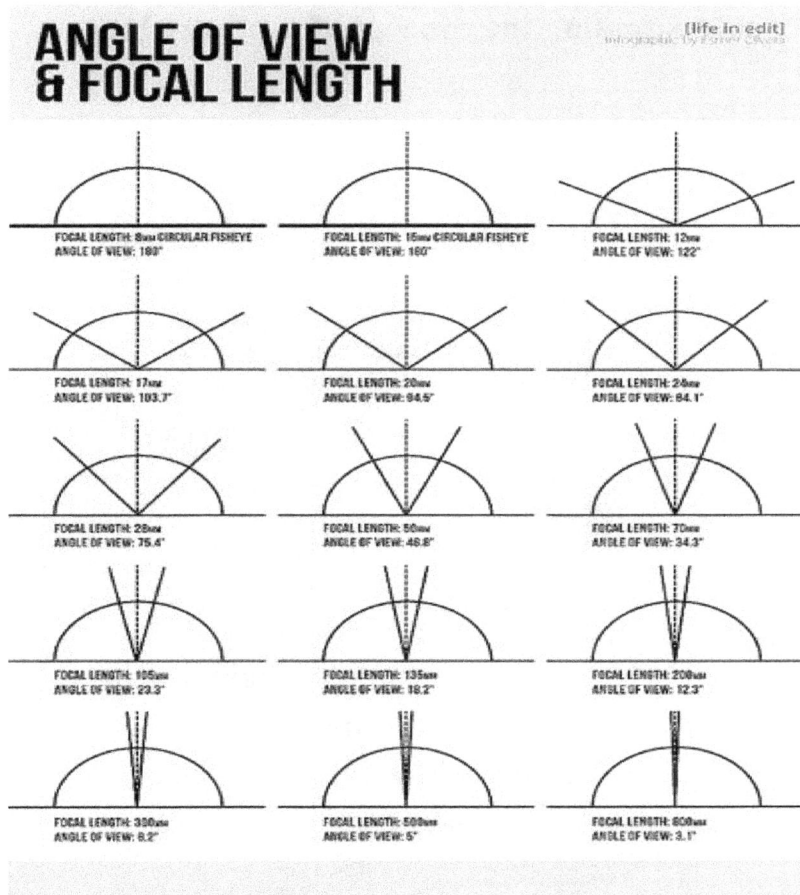

This is a term in photography that refers to the angle at which a camera views an object. The angle of view of a camera is not a function of the lens only but also includes the sensor. Since most digital sensors are small compared to a 35mm film, it will cause the lens to have an angle of view that is narrower than that of the film. The angle of view is also known as the field of view.

Understanding the concept of exposure latitude

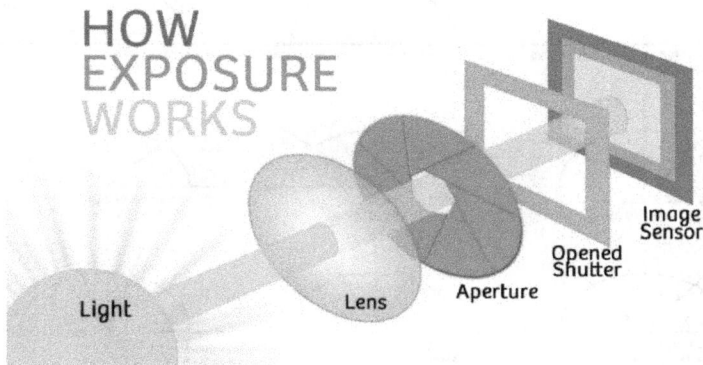

Exposure latitude refers to the permissible level of overexposing or underexposing a light-sensitive image without having a negative impact on its result. In photography, it is the difference between a camera's dynamic range and the dynamic range of the scene.

One of the factors used in determining latitude is the dynamic range. If you are able to use a camera to record a scene without using the full brightness available for the camera, it will shift the exposure along the range of brightness while you still maintain it in the highlight or shadow of the image. If the exposure latitude is large enough, it gives you room to compensate for exposure error without undermining the quality of the image.

Film laboratory and telecine

A film laboratory is an arm of the film industry which serves as a meeting point facility for industry specialists for the purpose of developing, printing, and ensuring that film materials are adapted for film production and distribution. The film material may be black and white, negative and positive, or of different film formats such as 35mm, 65mm, 16mm, and the rest.

One of the activities conducted at a film laboratory is telecine. Telecine refers to the process of converting motion picture into video for distribution to the consumers. Telecine is also an equipment used in the film industry in the post-production process.

The importance of telecine to the film industry is underscored by its ability to enable people to use equipment such as video cassette recorders, Bu-ray Disc, television sets, and computers to view images that are originally shot on film stock.

Author Dr Boniface Ikejiani

As a result, television producers, film producers, and film distributors can release their finished products on video for the general consumption of the people.

The use of color temperature in photography

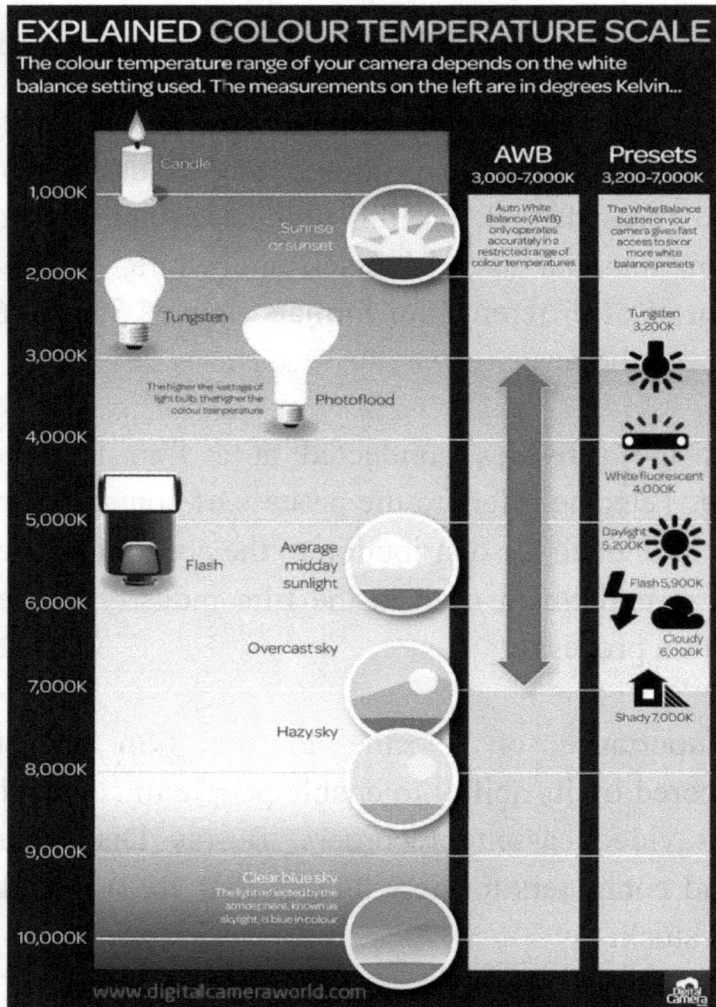

EXPLAINED COLOUR TEMPERATURE SCALE

The colour temperature range of your camera depends on the white balance setting used. The measurements on the left are in degrees Kelvin...

Author Dr Boniface Ikejiani

This is another important concept that will ensure that a picture is perfectly shot. The term refers to the measurement of light's color and is expressed in K or Kelvin. For instance, a candle will always produce reddish light. This color can be expressed with a number which is referred to as the color temperature.

Understanding the concept of color temperature will ensure that you always take accurate pictures that are devoid of unnatural colors. Now the question is, how does color temperature affect the quality of your images?

The human eye is designed to adjust and accommodate a variety of color temperatures. Therefore, we will always see an object as having the same color whether we are viewing it from outside or indoors under the same light bulb.

Digital cameras are not endowed with the same degree of adaptation as the human eye. Therefore, they "see" images in different colors. The color is usually determined by the lighting used. As a result of these differences, an image can have a color cast that will make the image appear unpleasing and unnatural.

Fortunately, cameras come with a feature that allows you to amend the color casts when you send the color temperature of the environment to the camera.

Author Dr Boniface Ikejiani

You can do this by taking advantage of the setting that allows you to tell the camera the nature of your scenes, such as shade, daylight, tungsten, and the rest. With the information supplied, the camera will use the right color temperature that will be ideal for the scene.

To increase the accuracy of control of the color temperature, some cameras are designed to allow you specify the specific color temperature in Kelvin. With the aid of a color meter, getting the accurate color temperature shouldn't be difficult for you.

You can equally shoot a white object that shares the same lighting with the object you want to shoot. The camera will use that to calculate the right color temperature based on the lighting of the white object.

You can easily balance color temperature by using two powerful tools. These tools are:

- **Color gel:** This is a colored material that is used in videography, theatre, and photography to correct color temperature. This transparent material is also known by other names such as color filter or lighting gel. Some of the color gels used for color correction are Color Temperature Orange (CTO) and Color Temperature Blue (CTB). The color gel works by altering the color temperature to a color that is close to the color temperature that the film negative uses. In the case of the CBT, it will alter the tungsten lights with a color temperature between 3,200k and 5,700k to a color that is close to Tungsten negative at about 5,400k. On the other hand, CTO will alter a color that is balanced by "Daylight" to be identical to the color temperature ideal for a Tungsten negative at about 3,200k.

• **Mired system:** Mired is contracted from micro reciprocal degree, and it is the unit of measurement of color temperature. The relationship between color temperature and the mired is expressed by this formula:

$M = 1,000,000/T$ where M is the desired mired value and T represents the color temperature expressed in Kelvin.

In photography, the term can be used to express the color temperature alteration that is done using a gel or filter for a specific light source and film.

Measuring light intensity

Whether you are in a studio or an outside location, you can measure the intensity of light by using light meters that are based on the principle of incidence and reflection. The two measurement options are discussed below:

• **Using incident light meters:** To measure light intensity with an incident meter, the meter is aimed directly at the

Author Dr Boniface Ikejiani

source of light and directly measures the light falling straight on the object. To ensure the accuracy of reading, any reflective tendency of the object is not allowed to influence the reading of the meter. If you desire a better control of the image, you should endeavor to measure from a good number of sources falling on different parts of the object to be photographed. Due to the ability to eliminate any external influences, this meter gives the most accurate reading.

• **Using reflected light meters:** Reflective reading is done by reading the intensity of the reflected light from an object. This may be affected by some factors such as nature of the surface of the object, contrast, color, shape, and other factors.
It should be noted that most light meters can easily take measurements in either reflective or incident mode.

The principles of electricity

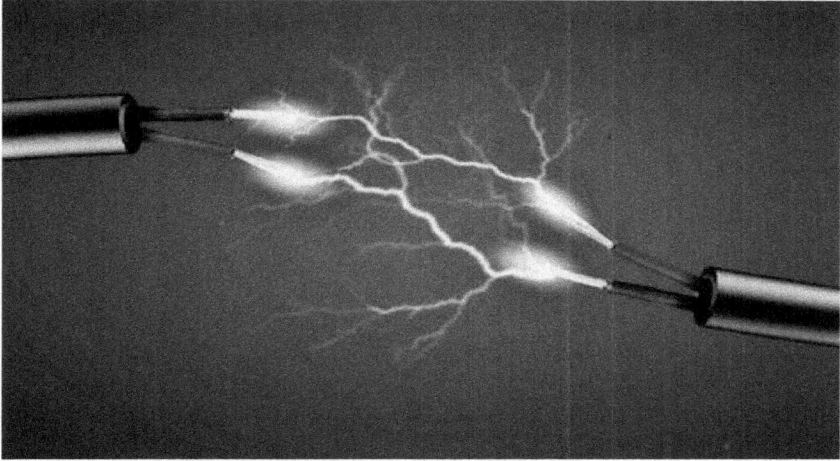

In the studio, the use electricity is extensively required. This is because nearly almost all the devices you will use for lighting and your camera, screens, and other devices make use of electricity. Therefore, a little knowledge of the principles of electricity will give you the basic knowledge of electricity and the preventive measures you can put in place to avoid possible dangers and challenges that can be posed by electricity.

To start with, the two most important factors when studying neurons (nerve cells that carry electrical impulse) are current and voltage. While the voltage is measured in volts, it is the measurement of the potential energy that is generated by two distinct charges. The value of the voltage is directly proportional to the potential differences between the two charges or points.

Current, on the other hand, represents the flow of electrical energy between two distinct points. This flow of energy is influenced by resistance and voltage. Resistance refers to the opposition to this flow of energy by an object, usually referred to as insulators.

Although the human body is a poor conductor, some factors or media, such as water, will increase the conductivity of the body. Therefore, a wet person is at a higher risk of exposure to electric shock.

To reduce your risk of electric shock whether, in the studio or other outdoor location, you should take these preventive measures:

- Learn about the basic principles of electricity.

- You should cover electrical outlets and sockets.

- Installing GFCI (Ground-fault Circuit Interrupter) breakers will also reduce your exposure to risk.

- Avoid getting wet.

Author Dr Boniface Ikejiani

- Call on licensed electrical technicians to handle any faulty electrical outlet or appliances.

- Before using an electrical outlet, have an expert check out for potential problems.

- Don't modify electrical plugs.

These are just a few of the precautionary measures you should take to prevent accidental shock or outright electrocution.

Television camera operations

The movie industry can choose from a wide range of television cameras at their disposal. In the lower end are cameras that can promise high-quality pictures under the best condition.

At the higher end, you will find expensive cameras with advanced features that make them churn out top-quality pictures regardless of the condition.

While the lower end cameras work better under optimum condition, the higher end can make the best use of a bad condition.

There are 6 basic camera types. These are:

1. Studio Broadcast Cameras

The studio cameras have these attributes:
- They are designed to be used in the studio only.

- They are heavy.

- They are used for multiple camera production (MCP).

- Studio cameras have large viewfinders which make them the favorite camera where excellent picture quality is required.

- They are connected to a studio wall and can be controlled by the Camera Control Unit located in the Outside Broadcast (OB) or the Production Control Unit (PCU).

2. Portable Broadcast Cameras

The portable broadcast camera can boast of the following features:
- It is compact and mobile.

- High-quality picture guaranteed.

- Can be used with a large viewfinder or zoom lens.

- It has different automated controls.

- It can be used for Single Camera Production (SCP) and Multiple Camera Production (MCP).

- It is a hybrid camera that can be detached for a wide range of purposes.

- It has a high-quality system which makes it useful for both outdoor and studio production.

3. Lightweight cameras

The characteristics of a lightweight camera include:
- It possesses a self-contained unit.

- It can be used for single camera production or SCP.

- It is designed for outdoor production.

- It is not as bulky as some other cameras.

- The camera can be attached to a tripod or hand-held as the need may be.

Author Dr Boniface Ikejiani

- It is battery-powered.

- The lightweight camera is fitted with its own Video Tape Recorder (VTR).

4. Hand-held low cost camera

This portable camera has these features:
- It is compact and hand-held.

- It can be used for industrial application.

- Its scope of use includes for CCTV (Closed Circuit TV).

- It can be connected directly to a VTR (Video Tape Recorder).

5. Combination Cameras

A combination camera has its unique characteristics which include:
- Compactness.

- Can be mounted on the shoulder or hand-held.

- Can be equipped with a recorder for recording both visual and sound.

- Immediate playback is possible.

- Has a range of form which includes the low budget type for photo enthusiasts and High-End Broadcast type for professional use.

6. Electronic Cinematography

An electronic cinematography camera is equipped with these attributes:
- It has detachable lenses.

- It can still use some other prime or film lenses.

- It can shoot images in video to be used as film.

The six cameras mentioned above are some of the best cameras in the movie industry. They are used for different purposes that will contribute to the overall high-quality image of a movie.

Author Dr Boniface Ikejiani

Television camera controls

A typical television camera has some controls. These are some of the common television camera controls:

- **Viewfinder:** The viewfinder is used to get the right focus for a camera prior to taking a shot. In some professional cameras, the viewfinders are in black and white. This is because the lens consumes less power than their counterparts with color viewfinders. You can adjust the viewfinder if there is a distinction between the scene you see on the television and that of your viewfinder.

- **Shutter:** All cameras have a shutter. It is the part of the camera that controls the amount of light that is allowed to pass through the camera at a point in time. The goal is to expose a light sensor to any source of illumination that will allow the camera to capture an image.

Television camera movement

When making videos, some camera movements are needed to capture the best image possible. Here are the basic moves used by experienced photographers to make high-quality images:

Author Dr Boniface Ikejiani

- **Tilt.**

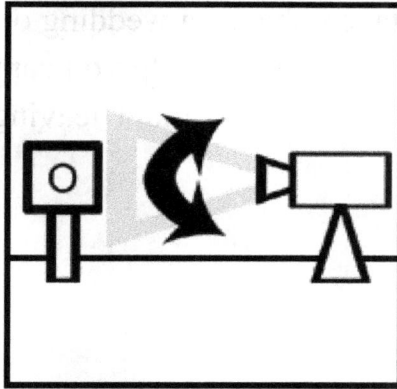

Tilting requires the photographer to keep the horizontal axis of the camera constant while moving the lens up or down. Tilting a camera is the fastest and the best way to shift from a high position to the low or vice-versa whenever you want to show two objects, although that may be at different times.

- **Pan.**

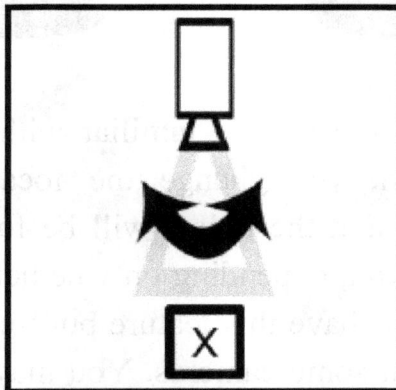

Author Dr Boniface Ikejiani

To Pan refers to move the lens to either the left or the right position. Panning is useful whenever you want to cover an audience. For instance, during a wedding or any show with a huge attendance, panning will help you capture the audience from one side to the other without leaving your stationary position.

- **Zoom**.

Nearly every camera user is familiar with this movement. When you zoom, you change the focal length of the camera's lens so that the object will be further away from you or closer to you, depending on whether you zoom in or out. Some cameras have this feature built-in while you need to manually zoom some cameras. You may use this feature to bring a distant object closer to you for a good shot or away from you as the case may be.

- **Pedestal.**

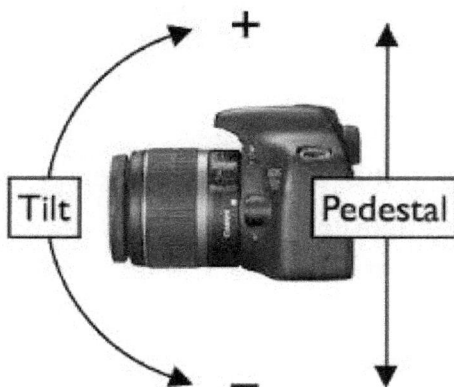

Pedestal refers to changing the camera's position up and down while both its horizontal and vertical axes remain stationary. Don't confuse this movement type with panning. When you pan, the camera's lens is moved to either the left or right position while pedestal refers to the movement of the camera up or down.

Author Dr Boniface Ikejiani

- **Dolly.**

Dolly is usually done when motion is directed towards an object or from an object. When you dolly in, you move towards the target while you move away from the object when you dolly out.

- **Truck.**

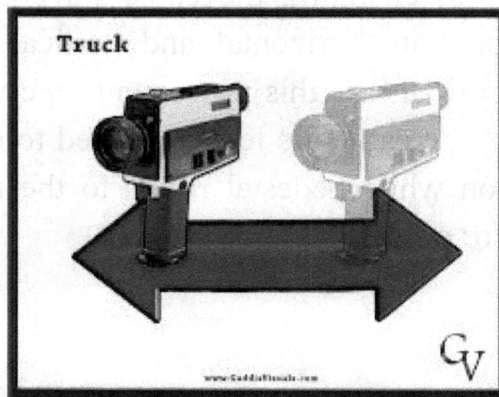

Trucking is similar to dollying. However, while dollying refers to a motion from or towards a subject, trucking refers

Author Dr Boniface Ikejiani

to any movement to the left or right of the subject. With trucking, you can easily capture someone as the person moves down the street. If you pan in this case, the person's back will be shown as he or she walks past the camera.

- **Crane.**

The crane move involves lifting a camera (and possibly together with its operator) with a crane. That allows the cameraman to move from a low shooting position to a high shooting position. Other related movement includes the jib that can be used for lifting a camera only. If you need an extreme lifting, you can use a drone for the same purpose.

Author Dr Boniface Ikejiani

The movements above are mostly the basic camera movements that are deployed for a wide range of roles in the movie industry. Since images of different locations and actions are taken, it is not strange that all the movements above can be combined when shooting a movie.

Career opportunities in the lighting and camera areas of the movie industry

If you are an experienced and licensed cameraman, there are different career opportunities for you to explore in the movie industry.

As a cameraman, you can play any of these roles in the movie industry:

• **Aerial camera assistant:** If you find yourself playing this role, you will be saddled with the responsibility of coordinating and rigging camera systems onto helicopters and other aircrafts for aerial filming. Your responsibilities generally involve, working with the other members of the crew to ensure the success of the production.

• **Camera operator:** As a camera operator, your job definition includes using TV, video, or other professional cameras for filming motion pictures in the movie industry. You must use your skills to ensure that the best narrative quality and scene composition are achieved.

Author Dr Boniface Ikejiani

As a cameraman, your job description includes operating the camera while you still maintain the composition of the shooting angle and the video framing.

You will also work together with the actors, director, actresses, and other crew members to get the best picture for a particular movie.

Due to your job description, you must have the right skills that will ensure the production of high-quality images. Therefore, you must be able to choose the best lenses for the cameras in the studio as well as choose the appropriate equipment such as technical props and tripods.

As a cameraman or a camera operator, you are an integral member of the film crew. Your input is crucial to the success of the movie. If you get it right, you will have a positive impact on the overall quality of a movie.

Otherwise, if you make some filming errors, the overall image of the movie will be affected negatively. Therefore, it is important that you combine expertise with professionalism when on the set of a movie.

This chapter has extensively discussed some of the basic concepts of camera operation. This is just one of the several areas that will be touched in this book.

Author Dr Boniface Ikejiani

Chapter 8

Lighting

The role of lighting in the Nigerian movie industry cannot be overemphasized. From the studio to the location, actors need a good dose of lighting to provide illumination for the crew whenever that is necessary.

The lighting department performs a wide range of functions and uses a wide variety of tools when carrying out these functions. These will be discussed in this chapter.

Author Dr Boniface Ikejiani

Lighting equipment and lamps

In the studio, there are different lighting equipment used by professional light men in the industry.

The lighting equipment used by these professionals goes beyond the ordinary bulbs and sockets we use at home. These are more powerful and technology-enhanced lighting equipment. Some of them are:

- **Bulb types**

In the movie industry, there a good number of bulb types. Most of these bulbs use the principle of filament-ignition for light production. This enables them to provide more powerful lighting than the general domestic lighting can possibly produce.

Some typical studio bulb types are:

- **Tungsten bulb:** This is a powerful lighting bulb. It provides more than 10 times what an average domestic bulb will produce. A single Tungsten bulb will produce between 1 kilowatt and 20 kilowatts of energy compared with the average of 100 watts produced by a domestic bulb.

This makes it the ideal bulb for lighting the interiors for video production. Some of its outstanding qualities include:

Author Dr Boniface Ikejiani

- It is inexpensive.
- Its color rendition is near perfect.
- It offers a better color temperature than the regular tungsten.
- It lasts longer than a regular incandescent.

- **HMI:** This is Hydrargyrum medium-arc iodide and is capable of giving between 85 and 108 lumens/watt. This is about four times what an average incandescent lamp will produce.

The HMI bulb can emit as much as 6,000K color temperature, a high-intensity light that closely matches that of the sunlight.

The awesome qualities of this particular bulb include:

- High color temperature.

- An impressive light output.

- It is more efficient than the traditional incandescent lamps.

The HMI light is used when there is a demand for high output. It can also be used whenever there is the need for augmenting or recreating sunlight in the interiors for lighting. Sometimes, it may be used for exterior lighting purposes. If the area of the illuminated is large, there are powerful HMI's specially made for that purpose.

- **Fluorescent:** Fluorescent lamps also produce light that is higher than what an average incandescent light can offer. It can generate as much as 100 lumens/watt. This is in the same range with what an HMI produces.

A fluorescent has a color temperature ranging between 2,700K and 6,500K. The value is determined by the concentration and quantity of phosphorus used.

Because fluorescent produce an even light that is equally soft, its area of application includes being used very close to the subject. It can also be used for illuminating the interiors because its light is cooler and more compact than lights from HMI and tungsten.

Lighting for scenery

Sometimes, there may be the need to arrange lighting for scenery. When the situation demands, some of the lighting instruments used are:

• **Fresnel:** This lighting instrument is directional. It is used most of the time as the key light when lighting scenery. It also has fast falloff which makes it to cast harsh shadows.

• **Flood light:** It is not as directional as Fresnel. Flood light makes soft shadows because of its slow falloff rate. However, it is the preferred choice when fill light is needed.

• **Elipsoidal:** This is the spotlight that is mostly used for special effects. It can be combined for some others such as gobos or cookies for the best result. It is a very directional light.

- **Cyc light:** Cyc light is mainly used for lighting backdrops.

Lighting for projections

It is sometimes necessary to light for projections. Some common technologies you should keep in mind when considering lighting for illuminations are:

- **Gobo:** This is an abbreviation of the phrase "Go Between Optics" in reference to the expected location of the disc in relation the path of light of a particular lighting fixture. This is a small circular disc, and is extensively used for creating a projected pattern or image in lighting. It is also use for providing visual interest for an image.

Author Dr Boniface Ikejiani

It has been found to be a better alternative to signage and banners that are used for corporate events so as to enable the audience have a good view of the object. The combination of the areas of application of Gobo makes it one of the best lighting options for projections.

- **Pin spot lighting:** Pin spotting is another way to give projections a good lighting that will enhance the visual impact of some objects. The pin spots refer to beams of white light that are usually projected on an object to make the objects stand out. This can be applied during the video of an object to increase its overall beauty and make it stand out.

- **LED strips:** This is a flexible circuit board that has light-emitting diodes incorporated. Its wide areas of use include but not limited to backlighting, accent lighting, and task lighting. Due to the low energy consumption of LED lights, they are used extensively in production videos. Other attributes of LED strips are that they are dimmable, can easily move around bend surfaces, and the ability to change color.

- **Projection mapping:** This is a video projector that can be used to map light onto a surface so that common objects can be changed into something awesome.

The roles perform by lighting makes it one of the most important areas that a construction crew must give undivided attention to in order to achieve the best result.

Author Dr Boniface Ikejiani

Chapter 9
Production Designing

A production designer is one of the earliest contributors to the success of a movie. He is actively involved in the pre-production stages of any movie. A production designer needs to be creative and have a flair for visual arts that sets him apart from the rest. Some of the roles of a production designer will be extensively discussed in this chapter.

What is production design?

David O. Selznick, a movie producer, coined this term and defined it as, "the creation and organization of the physical world surrounding a film story." It is sometimes referred to or otherwise called "scenic design" or "set design".

Author Dr Boniface Ikejiani

This involves designing the set for production, making location choices, and the supervision of the props. As simple as this definition is, a production designer's roles are defined by the demands of the film about to be produced. Sometimes, the designer may be responsible for everything about the outlook of a particular film while his or her roles may be drastically limited in other movies if the designer works together with the movie directors.

Specifically, a production designer is responsible for finding the perfect design style for the following:

- Lighting.

- Locations.

- Camera angles.

- Props.

- Costumes.

- Graphics.

- Sets.

In addition, the production designer also plays the following roles:

- He defines and manages all the aspects of a movie.

- He works with the Producer and Director to draft out a schedule and come up with the budget.

- He's responsible for directing the visual aspects of the movie, including costumes.

- He reads the scripts to identify some important factors that will help him understand the visual style needed for a movie.

- He discusses the production and concepts with the producer and director in order to understand the requirements for a particular movie.

- He plans and monitors everything about the design budget.

- He sources for the right materials that will make the production easier and with a positive impact on the movie.

- He is responsible for instructing the scenic artists, the set construction company, and the special effect artists to ensure that they put in their best.

Author Dr Boniface Ikejiani

- He liaises with the director of photography, costume designer, and the lighting, props, and sound directors.

- He checks the set during production to make sure that everything is in order and all the basic needs of the production crew are met.

He will play this role while working together with a producer or a director.

Impact of production design on production

It is evident that without production design, the production of a movie seems impossible. Without a competent production designer to see to the smooth running of the production, it may be flawed, leading to a negative rating. Therefore, the right concept needs to be decided, and a strong partnership should be formed between the production designer and the film director.

So many things may go out of hand that may affect the production in a different way. Therefore, it is important to realize that production design is an integral part of the production process.

Author Dr Boniface Ikejiani

Chapter 10
Sound recording

Sound is one of the most important elements of a good movie. If the sound recording is bad, the movie is as good as nothing. Without a good sound recording, the sound will be mingled and not distinct. This deficiency will defeat the purpose of the movie. Imagine watching a movie with bad sound recording.

Many equipments are used in the studio for sound recording. Some of them include:

Microphones

A microphone is a transducer equipped with the capability of converting electrical or mechanical energy into sound energy.

In recording today, two types of microphones are used in the recording studio. These are:

• **Dynamic microphones:** Dynamic microphones are known for their simple design. They also have few parts. They are sturdy and very strong and cannot be easily damaged by rough handling. Dynamic microphones are best used when high volume is required, especially from an amplifier or musical instruments. Dynamic microphones do not have internal amplifier and neither do they need any external power or batteries. They are versatile and can be used for a variety of purposes.

- **Condenser microphones:** These are the types of microphones that need an external source of light or to be powered by batteries. This gives it a stronger audio ability than one offered by dynamic microphones. They are also very responsive and sensitive. This makes them the ideal set of microphones for capturing some minor disturbances that are present in sound. Their stronger audio notwithstanding, condenser microphones are not designed for a heavy workload. This is due to their high sensitivity which also increases their susceptibility to distort.

Depending on the purpose, either of these two microphone types can be used in the studio for various functions.

Microphone polar patterns

Polar patterns are used in microphones to describe the way that microphones pick sound. These include where they pick the sound and the areas that are blocked.

Understanding the polar pattern will be useful in selecting the right microphone that will pick up the right sound while minimizing the impact of unwanted noise.

Author Dr Boniface Ikejiani

Some common microphone polar patterns are:

- **Cardioids microphones:** These microphones are perfect for capturing the sound in the rear (front) while everything else is blocked. Therefore, it is possible to point this microphone to the performer, capturing the sound while eliminating any ambient sound.

This makes it one of the best microphones for live performance and other areas where there is the need to minimize the impact of interferences and suppress feedback.

Cardioids microphones are the most popular microphones used for live performances in arena concerts and the likes. Some other notable uses of the mic include amplifying the sounds of guitar speakers and drum kits.

Hyper/super cardioids microphone: These microphones share the same directionality with cardioids microphones but do not boast of the same degree of sensitivity. Although they both capture sound from the rear, these microphones' area of sensitivity is narrower than that of the cardioids. The result is a better isolation and the ability to resist feedback than the cardioids microphones.

Due to the improved degree of resistance to external influence, they are the best microphones for sound sources with loud output, noisy stage, or recording rooms.

Author Dr Boniface Ikejiani

Omnidirectional microphones: These microphones can capture sound from any angle or direction. As the design of these microphones makes room for capturing sound from any direction and have zero rejection, they have better ability to capture nuances, making their outputs the best thing closest to natural sound.

They can be used in studios and other places that boast of great acoustics.

Shotgun microphones: These are otherwise known as Line and Gradient. Their design makes them have more directional capturing ability than the hyper cardioids. They use the principle of phase cancellation to eliminate unwanted sound from both sides of the microphone. This makes their polar pattern to be tighter in the front position and have a pickup range that is higher than that of others.

As a result, the shotgun microphones are good for capturing sounds from chorals, singing groups, and drum cymbals.

Therefore, choosing the right microphone depends on the purpose the mic will serve.

Microphone techniques used in studio recording

Using different microphone techniques in the studio makes it possible for you to achieve different range of sounds while recording. This may be helpful considering that you must produce sounds to meet a wide variety of needs.

Although to the uninitiated, a single recording technique is used for recording instruments and vocals, but there are different microphone techniques you can use for recording. Some of these techniques include:

Close Mic Placement

This is the commonest microphone placement technique. This technique requires placing the mic about three feet from the source of sound to ensure that a close and audible recording is possible.

By using this technique, you have a better chance at reducing the external interferences you picked from the environment. This results in a better sound quality. It also makes adding effects, processing, and mixing your sound easier as the recording will be direct and dry.

Author Dr Boniface Ikejiani

The technique also makes it possible to separate sounds if your recordings are from different sources so that you can easily minimize leakage from each of the audio sources.

Distant Mic Placement

This technique requires placing the microphone more than three feet away from the sound source. This results in picking ambient sound from the room.

If the studio had a great setup, the output from this natural ambient sound will be great and will have a positive impact on the quality of the sound.

However, it will be a better option if you can use the close mic method for the recording and then add the appropriate reverb later. This will make the process of achieving a good mix and production much easier since you can use the same reverb for all other recordings.

Alternatively, you can consider the idea of recording with two microphones. This is possible if you want to:

• Combine the signals from the two microphones to make the sound more powerful.

• To blend the two sounds together if you want to alter the tone.

Author Dr Boniface Ikejiani

• To select from a list of stereo microphone techniques with the objective of creating the real stereo of the sound.

A typical example of using two microphones is when you decide to use a condenser mic and a dynamic mic together and later mix the recordings for the production of the desired sound. This is exemplified during the recording of guitar amps.

It is very easy to use any of the techniques discussed above for the recording of instruments or vocals you intend using when producing music. The choice of technique is simply yours and that will be determined by what you are recording and the type of sound you wish to produce.

How to choose the right microphones

Although there are a variety of microphones that you can choose from for your recording works, it is ideal to find a way of identifying the right microphone for a particular recording. Some of the factors we need to consider include:

• **Sound Pressure Level (SPL):** This refers to the dynamic level or range the microphone can handle. It is a measure of the range of volume it can deal with without the threat of low noise when the microphone is at low level or the problem of distortion if it is working at high level. In this area, dynamic mics are better than others when used for recording from a loud sound source.

- **Noise level or noise floor:** This is a measure of the level of background noise that the microphone itself produces. When considering this factor, Capacitor mics have proved to be better than dynamic mics at capturing nuances and subtleties.

- **Sensitivity:** In a simple term, the sensitivity is a measure of the loudness capacity of a microphone. Different microphones have different sensitivities, making them useful for a variety of purposes.

- **Polar patterns:** The polar pattern of a microphone is also another important factor to be considered when choosing the right microphone. It refers to the direction at which the sound is picked as already discussed above. Generally, there is no specific rule guiding the best pattern for recording vocals. Nevertheless, most sound engineers have a thing for a condenser mic with a cardiod pattern while some people have a strong argument for the omni pattern.

When you put all these factors into consideration, you can easily make the right choice of microphone, and that will have a positive impact on the quality of your sound.

Author Dr Boniface Ikejiani

How will a room's design affect the sound and feel of a recording?

The acoustical conditions of a recording room have a powerful effect on the sound quality from the room.

These are some acoustical problems that can affect the sound quality:

• **Reverberation:** Reverberation refers to the spaced reflections on the studio's boundaries. Reverberation is known for extending sound and can have a mask effect on the quality of the sound. While the recommended Reverberation time (RT60) is between 0.2 to 0.4 second in an untreated studio, RT60 can fall between 0.5 to 1.5 seconds.

• **Lateral reflections:** Lateral reflections can have a negative effect on the quality of a sound. These reflections create fake sources of sound outside the sound source, leading to an increase in the stereo image. As a result, the sound element shared between the used speakers are enlarged and thus, affects the quality of sound produced by the speakers.

• **Direct to reverberant ratio:** This refers to the difference between reverberated and direct sound levels. If the ratio is weak, it will have a negative impact on the quality of the sound. If the ratio is too strong, it also poses a negative effect on the sound quality as well.

The combination of these factors will affect the quality of sound produced in a sound studio, either positively or negatively.

It is important that this department is at the top of its game to effectively contribute to the success of the production.

Chapter 11
Music/Sound track production

- What is music/sound track production?

Music/soundtrack refers to the music used in a movie or a television show, or in an album sold containing that music. Sometimes, the music has been recorded just for the film or album and often depending on the type of movie, the soundtrack album will contain portions of music composed for dramatic effect.

- The importance of music/sound track production.

A good soundtrack is something that becomes instantly memorable, recognizable and at times, even bigger than the film itself. Soundtrack is an important part of cinema because it can help a film become instantly memorable.

- Music/sound track production software programs.

1. Ableton Live
2. FL Studio
3. Apple Logic Pro
4. Avid Pro Tools
5. Propellerhead Reason
6. Apple GarageBand
7. Sony Acid
8. Steinberg Cubase
9. Cockos Reaper
10. PreSonus Studio

- Music/sound track equipment.

1. Microphones
2. Mixers
3. Amplifiers
4. Speakers
5. PA systems
6. Instruments
7. Accessories (cables, stands, power conditioners, woofers, drivers, etc.)

Author Dr Boniface Ikejiani

Chapter 12
Still photography

Still photography is a genre of photography used in the depiction of non-moving photographs. It plays a very important role in the production of movies. This chapter will discuss some important areas of still photography, how cameras work, lighting, and other important areas of still photography.

Author Dr Boniface Ikejiani

Camera modes and uses

Most digital cameras used in the movie industry support a good number of modes which makes them versatile for use for different situations.

Some of the most important camera modes and their uses are discussed below:

1. Automatic mode

This is the mode that most digital camera users are familiar with. The auto mode is designed to give the camera the freedom to make the best decision when it comes to selecting the right aperture, shutter speed, ISO, focus, white balance, and flash when taking a shot. When used in different shooting conditions, the auto mode has proved very valuable.

Author Dr Boniface Ikejiani

2. Portrait mode

Switching to the portrait mode will cause your camera to make an automatic selection of a large aperture so that your background can be kept out of focus. This will allow your subject to be the only image in focus. You will get the best result from this mode if you want to shoot a single subject as you can easily move closer to the subject, either by walking closer to the subject or zooming in.

3. Macro mode

Author Dr Boniface Ikejiani

This mode allows you to get closer to your subject to allow you have the best shot. It is the best mode for shooting small subjects such as insects, flowers, and other tiny elements.

4. Landscape mode

SHUTTER SPEED: 1/100   APERTURE: F/16   ISO SPEED: 100   FLASH: NOT FIRED

While the portrait mode works on a large aperture, landscape mode is the very opposite of that as it uses a small aperture to make sure that most of the scene you are shooting are in focus. So, if you are considering capturing images of wide scenes, especially if you have different areas of interest that are at different distances from you, landscape mode is the ideal choice. Sometimes, the camera may decide to use a slow shutter speed as compensation for the small aperture. Therefore, you may consider using a tripod to ensure the stability of the camera.

Author Dr Boniface Ikejiani

5. Sports mode

The sports mode is designed for capturing moving objects. When a scene involves cars, pets, wildlife, or sports, the sports mode is the ideal mode for the best shot.

6. Night mode

This is an exciting mode. You can use it to create some interesting and colorful shots. This mode, otherwise called slow shutter sync, is the ideal mode for shooting when the light situation is low as it sets the camera to long shutter speed so that you can easily capture the background. It also illuminates the subject and foreground to give you the best shooting option. It is advisable that you use a tripod in order to have a good background and prevent a blurred background.

7. Movie mode

The movie mode makes it possible for the user to capture moving objects. Most modern digital cameras come with this feature and can capture both sound and video too.

8. Aperture priority mode

This is a semi-automatic mode that allows you to make aperture choice while the camera will decide the other settings such as white balance, shutter speed, ISO, and so on. This mode is useful for controlling the depth of the field and the degree of the scene that will be in focus.

9. Shutter priority mode

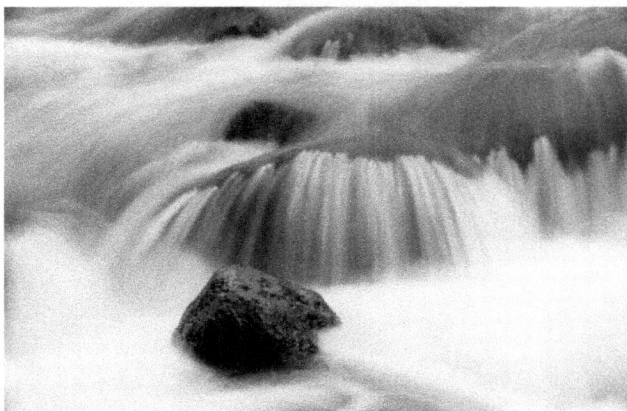

Author Dr Boniface Ikejiani

This mode shares some similarities with the aperture priority mode except that it allows you to select the shutter speed while the other settings are left to the discretion of the camera itself. This is the ideal mode if you have the desire to control the shutter speed yourself. For instance, it is used whenever you want to shoot a moving subject, and you may want to select a fast shutter speed for freezing motion effect. You may also want to shoot a movement such as a waterfall and select a shutter to create a blurred movement. Whenever the light situation is low, you may consider choosing a shutter speed that is slow.

10. **Manual code**

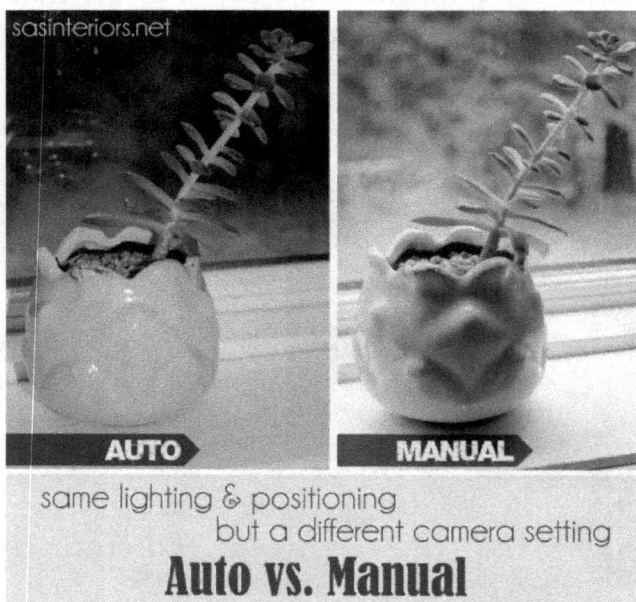

same lighting & positioning
but a different camera setting
Auto vs. Manual

Author Dr Boniface Ikejiani

This mode makes it easy to manually control your camera so that all the settings including aperture, shutter speed, white balance, ISO, and flash will be manually selected. This total control allows you the flexibility of setting your shot as it pleases you.

ISO settings in Digital Photography

ISO 200   ISO 400   ISO 800   ISO 1600

In digital photography, ISO refers to the level of sensitivity of a film to light or the image sensor. The setting is numbered on the film for different purposes. The sensitivity of a film is dependent on this number because high ISO settings mean higher sensitivity while lower number equally means lower sensitivity of your camera to light and the finer the grain.

Author Dr Boniface Ikejiani

Therefore, if you increase the ISO of a camera from 100 to 200, the camera sensitivity will be automatically doubled, and vice versa.

In dark situations, higher ISO settings are ideal for use as they ensure that you have faster shutter speeds. The preferred ISO setting according to most professionals is 100 ISO because this setting gives you the best shot with little grain or noise.

If you want to be able to fully control your digital camera, you must be able to understand this concept. You may find it useful to experiment with a variety of ISO settings and their impact on your images. While at it, concentrate on the shutter speed and the aperture. This will give you mastery over the subject and how to use it to your benefit.

Focusing options

In photography, focus is practically connected to sharpness. It is equivalent or married to the level of sharpness of an image. An image that is completely sharp is said to be in-focus. While shooting a movie, it may be important to shoot different scenarios in order to get shots in-focus.

This requires that you use a variety of focusing options to get the best shot of the subject.

Author Dr Boniface Ikejiani

In photography, there are a couple of these options to choose from. A couple of the photography options are:

- **One shot mode:** This is the best shooting option when the subject is stationary. Some examples of such circumstances include still life, architecture, and landscape. The rule of thumb is that if the subject is not moving, go for One Shot Mode for your shot. While in this mode, your subject will be oblivious of any movement.

- **Al Focus Mode:** This mode combines One Shot Mode and Al Servo. This is the perfect focus mode when you must take images of both moving and static objects. When using this mode, the camera automatically determines the best mode for an image and switches into the mode promptly. An example is at a wedding where you may need to shoot a picture of a moving object. The camera is design to personally determine the absence or presence of movement and act accordingly.

- **Manual mode:** If you turn the auto focusing feature of your lens off by switching the lens to MF mode from AF mode, you will have access to the manual mode. In some situations, it may be helpful to switch the auto focus off, particularly when the auto focus finds it challenging to focus on the subject in a dark room. You can also find switching the auto focus off whenever you want to take some awesome shots with blur.

Author Dr Boniface Ikejiani

Valuable composition tips

Getting a good shot goes beyond owing a camera only. You must apply some simple but effective composition tips that will help you get the right shot. These tips are:

- **Obey the rule of thirds**

This rule requires that you place your point of interest on some imaginary intersections. According to the rule, you should imagine your image as being divided into nine equal segments by 2 horizontal and 2 vertical lines. The most important part of your image should be at the point of intersections of the lines.

- **Balance the elements**

When you obey the rule of third, you will have an amazing picture. There is a little problem, though: that may leave the scene with a void that can make the scene feel empty. You should endeavor to balance your object's "weight" by filling the empty space with another object, although, with lesser importance compared to your main subject.

- **Consider viewpoint**

Whenever you want to take a photograph, learning to consider the viewpoint is a great photography practice. Rather than simply take a shot from eye level, you should consider trying some shooting angles. You should consider taking the picture from the side, ground level, high above, close up, and other alternatives to the eye level. This will have a positive impact on the quality of your image.

- **The background is important**

The background may play an important role in the quality of your photo. By the virtue of the human eye, it can easily differentiate between the different elements present in a scene. While a camera may flatten the background and foreground or make them visible, either way, it may have a dire consequence on the quality of the photo. You can correct this problem while shooting by using an unobtrusive and plain background and placing your image in the right position so that the background doesn't detract or distract from your subject.

- **Depth**

Due to the two-dimensional nature of photography, you should choose the best composition that will convey the same sense of depth conveyed by the actual sense.

You can do this by capturing the objects in the middle ground, foreground, and background of the subject. You may also consider overlapping the images, a technique that requires partially obscuring an object with another. The layers between the overlapped objects can easily be recognized by the human eye. The mental separation of the object will create an awesome image with the ideal depth.

Author Dr Boniface Ikejiani

- **Frame the object**

If you look around you, you will find natural objects that can serve as frames for your subjects. Some of these objects are archways, trees, and holes. When you place these objects around the edge of your subject, you can easily isolate the subject, giving you a perfect image.

- **Center dominant eye**

If you want to create the impression that your human subject follows you with his or her eyes, simply center the dominant eye. The impact on the image will be awesome.

Night photography

Shooting at night can be quite challenging, especially if you are not accustomed to it. However, you can get a good shot at night if you have these photography equipment:

- **Tripod:** Although you may not always need a tripod, the flexibility it gives you to get the right angles cannot be overemphasized. While you keep your camera steady while trying to get a good shot, the tripod stand will provide a helping hand.

- **Wide-angle lenses:** Wide-angle lenses will help you overcome some of the challenges that are peculiar to night photography. They are lens whose focal length is significantly smaller than the focal length of a normal lens

Author Dr Boniface Ikejiani

for a given film plane. These lenses gives you the privilege to have more of the scene included in the shot. You can check for a list of wide-angle lenses that will give you the best result.

• **A lens hood:** You need this for minimizing the impact of lens flares from affecting the quality of your image.

• **A flashlight:** You may need this whenever you want to lighten up any dark part of the foreground or draw attention to something.

• **Your imagination:** You need your imagination to get out of some tight corner at times. Look around you and you will find the perfect tool that will make it easy for you to get the best out of the photography, regardless of how dark the scene is.

Intro to lighting

There are different ways to introduce lighting to a photographic shooting. Some basic concepts involved in this are:

Drive modes

The drive modes are responsible for the frequency of taking a picture. There are five Drive modes and they include:

- **Single shot:** This is the most frequently used mode where you take a single shot of the subject. Immediately the shutter button is pressed, the image will be immediately captured while the shutter is ready to take another shot. Since this mode can be used for capturing any type of image, from landscapes to portraits, it is used more often than other modes.

- **Continuous shooting:** When you are using the continuous shooting mode, you only need to hold down the shutter while your camera will capture images repeatedly. The camera type determines how many images can be captured per second. Some professional cameras can shoot as much as 8 or more per second while the Nikon 1 is known for taking up to 60 frames/second. The continuous shooting mode is great for capturing any object in motion. You can also use it to create portraits that you can use later to form a triptych. After capturing the action, you may need to wait for a while for the camera to process the shots.

- **Self-timer:** With the self-timer options, you can press the shutter down without taking a photograph. Self-timing a camera can serve multiple purposes. If it is necessary for the

Author Dr Boniface Ikejiani

photographer to appear in the picture, the shutter will be pressed down while the photographer joins the subject. On the other hand, it can also be used for the prevention of camera shake. When pressing the shutter, the camera will shake a bit. With the self-timer, the shaking would have been corrected before the camera eventually takes shot.

- **Mirror up:** In SLR-type cameras, the processes for shooting a picture make the camera vulnerable to slight vibrations. This is not an ideal situation for taking good pictures, especially when the photography isn't ready immediately or whole and you have to work in low light. When you lock the mirror up, the slight vibration will be stopped to prevent it from affecting the quality of the image due to its vibration.

- **Multiple exposures:** This refers to taking more than an image on a single frame. After taking the first shot, it doesn't move into the memory but rather waits for you to take the second shot. The second image is now set on the first one so that both of them now bind together to form a single image. Although this feature is not available in all cameras, you can take single shots and do the rest with image-editing software like Photoshop.

Author Dr Boniface Ikejiani

White balance

White balance is one of the best features of photography for experienced photographers who understand the concept. It is applied to get the colors in the images as accurate as possible.

Simply put, white balance is needed in photography to make it easy for you to get the right color in your image. This is important because different light sources have different color temperatures too. As a result, an object may appear to have different colors when viewed under different lights.

For instance, if you view an object under fluorescent lighting, the fluorescent will give it a bluish cast whereas incandescent light will add a yellow cast to the object. Therefore, if you view this object under these different lightings, they won't give you the same result. Therefore, white balance allows you to make the necessary adjustment so that the real color of an object will come out regardless of under the lighting it is viewed in.

While that doesn't pose a problem to humans because the human eye is endowed with the accommodation feature, the same cannot be said of cameras. They will notice the differences and produce the result according to what they "see."

Author Dr Boniface Ikejiani

If the light is cool (such as green or blue), you need to ask the camera to increase the temperature. Otherwise, the camera should cool it down in warm light.

Adjusting white balance

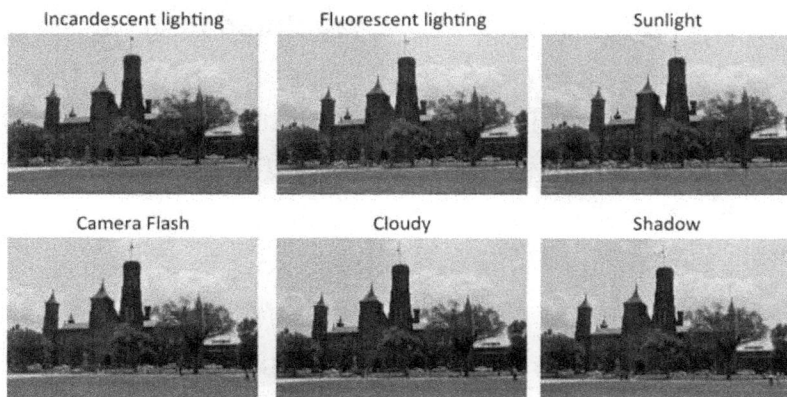

Incandescent lighting · Fluorescent lighting · Sunlight

Camera Flash · Cloudy · Shadow

Adjusting the white balance differs from one camera to the other. To understand how to adjust the white balance in your camera, you may have to consult your instructions manual. This camera's manual will guide you on how to make the necessary white balance changes.

However, many digital cameras are equipped with either semi-automatic or automatic modes that will prove helpful in changing the white balance.

Author Dr Boniface Ikejiani

If you have either of the modes in your camera, you can find the following White Balance settings:

- **Auto:** The auto setting gives the camera the freedom to make the necessary adjustment based on each shot taken. In many situations, the auto setting has proved invaluable in helping photographers to make automatic white balance adjustment for the benefit of their captured images.

- **Tungsten:** A small bulb is usually used to symbolize this mode. The tungsten mode is useful for indoor shootings, especially if the subject is under incandescent (tungsten) lighting. This mode cools down the colors in a photo.

- **Fluorescent:** Due to the coolness of a fluorescent light, the mode is very useful in compensating for the coolness by warming up any shot you take with the camera while in this mode.

- **Daylight/Sunny:** This setting sets the white balance setting in "normal." So, it is not common to all cameras.

- **Cloudy:** The Cloudy setting has a little more impact on the white setting than the "dailylight" setting. It warms up the shot a bit.

- **Flash:** A camera's flash can also have a positive impact on the color quality of an image. The Flash White Balance setting will also warm up the shots to give it a better quality.

- **Shade:** The Shade settings will also warm up your shots a bit. It provides a cooler impact than shooting the subject in direct sunlight.

Adjusting white balance manually

The white balance modes above are preset and can give you an accurate result.

However, most digital cameras (such as most DSLRs) offer you the opportunity to manually set the white balance.

Although the mode of operation of the manual white balance adjustment is a bit different from one model to the other, the general principle involves telling your camera how a white shot looks like. This gives the camera a reference point that will be valuable in helping the camera determine what colors will complement the reference point to give you the desired result.

To find the right reference point for the camera, buy a grey or white card that is designed for this particular purpose.

Author Dr Boniface Ikejiani

Once you find out how it can be done manually on your camera, you will find it very easy to set. If you don't have the knowledge of white balance, it is advisable to learn it. Your success in Nollywood as a photographer depends on your ability to deliver top-notch jobs.

Exposure compensation

If you are a seasoned photographer, you must have a good knowledge of this concept to improve your output and create a niche for yourself in the movie industry.

Exposure compensation refers to a feature on cameras that will make it possible for you to increase the darkness or lightness of an object. This feature allows you to get a good shot despite the light quality of the scene, either high-light or low-light. When it would have been practically impossible to take a shot in areas like that, compensating for exposure will help you to have a good shot.

The exposure compensation icon is +/-. The plus sign setting can be used to make a light object lighter while the minus mark can be used to darken an already dark image.

Most cameras are incorporated with this feature and that is one of the many factors that allow most cameras to perform wonderful well when taking pictures with different exposures. Now that you are conversant with exposure compensation, how can you use it?

You will use the +/- button to specify the type of compensation that you want. While you are pressing the button, simultaneously turn the dial beside your shutter button right or left. As you turn the dial to your desired direction, the exposure compensation will be changed. Turning the dial in one direction will increase the exposure while turning it in the opposite position will lead to a reduction in the exposure.

In some higher-end DSLR, your camera will come with a wheel or second dial that can be used in lieu of the +/- button that is absent in the camera. Without having to press any button, you just use the second dial to change the exposure compensations.

Application of basic elements of composition

Lenses and Filters

Most camera users are of the opinion that filters are fitted to a lens primarily for protecting the lens. While that may not be absolutely wrong because filters protect the lens against moisture, dust, and thumb print, they are designed to improve the quality of the pictures you take with the camera.

The basic filters are UV reducing filters, protection filters, and skylight filters. These filters are either glass or regular UV filters that are plainclothes depending on the filter brand and manufacturer.

UV Filters

UV filters are designed to overcome the effect of moisture, atmospheric haze, and other airborne pollutants that are known for causing image degradation. These filters, also known as Haze filters, are in different forms with varying degrees of strengths.

If you intend photographing objects at high altitudes, bodies of water, in the snow, or in other related conditions that may magnify the influence of ultra-violet light, it is advisable that you use UV filtrations that offer the greatest resistance to the

Author Dr Boniface Ikejiani

impact of these elements. Some examples of such high-level UV filtration are UV-410, UV-415, UV-420, UV-Haze 2A, UV-Haze 2B, UV-Haze 2C, and UV-Haze 2E.

UV filters can have an amber-like appearance and also warm. Their exposure composition requirement is from zero to almost a half stop.

Skylight filters

Skylight filters are the best alternative to the UV filters. They are available as Skylight A1 and Skylight 1B, depending on their degree of strength. Skylight filters have a distinct appearance to the UV filters. While the former is known for their warm amber appearance, the latter are known for their magenta tint. Skylight filters are the preferred choice if you want to use color slide film or photograph skin tones.

Regardless of the Skylight filter's strength, they generally have zero effect on the exposure level of the camera. However, they have a similar impact on dust, atmospheric haze, fingerprints, and moisture as UV filters do.

Chapter 13
Video editing

Video editing is the process of editing segments of motion video production footage, special effects and sound recordings in the post-production process. It involves the process of taking video recorded, and delete or remove clips of that recorded video that are not necessary or needed in the story.

- Why video editing is needed in the movie industry?

Video editing is one of the most important steps in creating the final cut of a movie. Video editing is the key to blending images and sounds and make the viewer feel emotionally connected and sometimes truly there, in the film he's watching.

- Best video editing software programs.

The best video editing software programs are:
1. Adobe Premiere Pro CC
2. Corel VideoStudio Ultimate X10
3. Apple Final Cut Pro X
4. CyberLink PowerDirector
5. Punnacle Studio Ultimate
6. Apple iMovie
7. Avid Media Composer

Chapter 14
Sound Recording

- History of sound recording.

All of the experiments in capturing sound on a recording medium for preservation and reproduction began during the Industrial Revolution of the 1800s. Many attempts to record and reproduce sound were made during the latter half of the 19th century and all these efforts culminated in the invention of phonograph by Thomas Edison in 1877.

There are four main periods of sound recording:

1. The "Acoustic" era (1877-1925).
2. The "Electrical" era (1925-1945).
3. The "Magnetic" era (1945-1975).

Author Dr Boniface Ikejiani

4. The "Digital" era (1975-present).

- Sound recording software.

1. Ableton live
2. Apple logic pro x
3. Cubase
4. Fruity loops
5. Magix music maker
6. Pro tools
7. Reaper
8. Reason

- Sound recording equipment.

Sound recording is a really important part of filmmaking industry. The equipment used in sound recording include:
1. Lavalier microphone
2. Wireless microphones
3. Directorial microphones
4. Audio recorder

- Sound recording app.

1. Audio recorder
2. Call recorder
3. Easy voice recorder
4. Hi-Q mp3 voice recorder

Author Dr Boniface Ikejiani

5. Parrot
6. RecForge II
7. Smart voice recorder
8. Snipback
9. Voice recorder Pro

Author Dr Boniface Ikejiani

Chapter 15
Subtitling

- Why are movies subtitled?

Subtitles in movies are used because they may be understood better, they may be used for deaf persons and also they are used for persons that do not understand foreign languages.

Author Dr Boniface Ikejiani

- Subtitling rules.

1. Editing
2. Timing
3. Subtitle breaks
4. Keeping in sync

- Subtitling apps.

1. Subtitle edit
2. Visual Sub Sync
3. Subtitle workshop
4. Subtitle creator
5. Aegisub Advanced Subtitle Editor
6. DivXLand Media Subtitler
7. WinSubMux
8. Subtitle editor
9. AHD Subtitles Maker
10. SubEdit Player

- Best subtitling companies.

1. Caption Technologies Inc.
2. Accent Network
3. Aphatrad North America
4. Moving Words

Author Dr Boniface Ikejiani

Chapter 16
Lip Synchronization

Lip Sync Mouth Positions

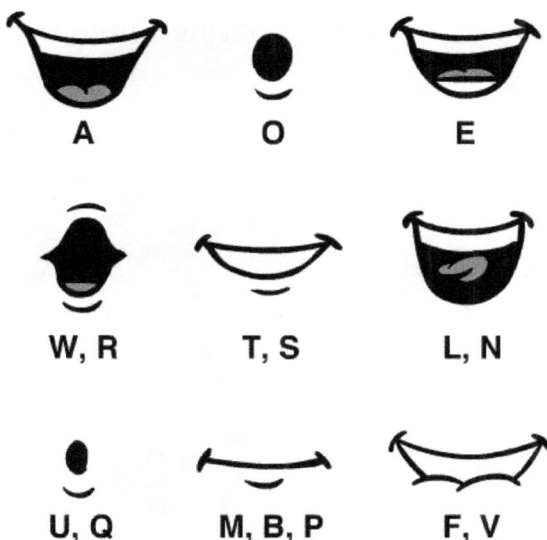

A	O	E
W, R	T, S	L, N
U, Q	M, B, P	F, V

- What is lip synchronization?

Lip synchronization or lip sync is a technical term for matching a speaking or singing person's lip movements with prerecorded sung or spoken vocal that listeners hear, either through the sound reinforcement system in a live

Author Dr Boniface Ikejiani

performance or via television, computer or cinema speakers in other cases.

- The importance of lip synchronization in movies.

Lip synchronization in movies is important when films are dubbed into other languages. In many musical movies, actors sang their own songs beforehand in a recording session and lip synchronized it during filming.

Chapter 17
Voice over/Voice talent

- Who is a voice over artist?

A voice over artist is a voice talent specialist who is reading from a script and may appears elsewhere in the production.

- Voice over jobs.

1. Audiobooks
2. Movie trailers

Author Dr Boniface Ikejiani

3. Business Presentations and Corporate Videos
4. Podcasting
5. Cartoons
6. Radio Commercials
7. Documentaries
8. Telephone
9. Educational Videos
10. Television
11. Internet
12. Videogames

- Best voice over software.

Adobe Audition

- Why is a voice over needed?

A voice over is important in the makeup of filmmaking, most especially in this new age. In the Digital Age, it knows when to move inflection points, when to pull at emotions, and when to simply deliver a clean message. A good voice over has lots of benefits such as:
1. Giving video the required credibility.
2. It's a great filler.
3. Humanizes things.
4. It's persuasive.

Chapter 18
Speech doctoring

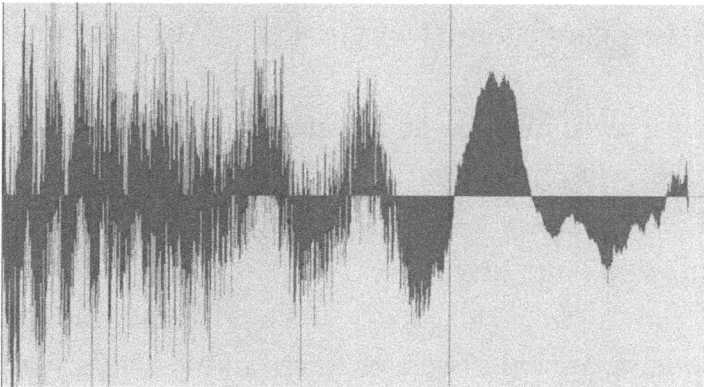

- What is speech doctoring?

Speech doctoring is more about speech editing. Doctoring a speech refers to transforming it from something simple into something complex, appealing and memorable. Editing a speech is a plus because all of the topics that are going to be covered will reach out to attract more audience and make the speech interactive and attractive.

Author Dr Boniface Ikejiani

- How is speech doctored?

1. Edit for focus – al elements of the speech must support the core message.
2. Edit for clarity – ordering the speech logically is one of the best ways to ensure clarity.
3. Edit for concision – eliminate all of the unessential elements.
4. Edit for continuity – avoid abrupt transitions which can lose audience members.
5. Edit for variety – variety makes the speech more enjoyable and engaging.
6. Edit for impact and beauty – surprise the audience with vivid images, appeal of senses, memorable lines.

- Top best speech doctoring software.

Adobe VoCo (voice conversation) software.

Chapter 19
Choreography/Dance Instructing/Dancing

- What is choreography?

Choreography is the art of designing sequences of movements and steps, in figure skating, ballet or other staged dance.

- Dance instructing

Dance instructing is an act carried out by someone called a choreographer and he is the one who created choreography.

Author Dr Boniface Ikejiani

- Why is choreography important in filmmaking?

It is needed to interpret the movement of physical bodies in filmmaking industry as an abstract concept. The art of film has to be acknowledged as deeply involved with choreography in its essence.

- What is the importance of dance instructing?

Similar to acting, dancing has a lot of importance in everybody's life because it can teach early learners to think and respond to the world around them, it gives freedom and permission to question and explore, and it also demands focus. Through dancing, we can get to know ourselves better (mind, body, spirit), it demands to set goals and directs people to depend on themselves, and also keeps people moving.

Author Dr Boniface Ikejiani

Chapter 20
Special Effect

- What is special effect?

A special effect is described as the illusion or trick of the eye that are used in cinema, television, theater and video games to stimulate events imagined in a story or in a virtual world.

- How is special effect done?

Special effects in movies are not all done with computers. Fake snow, artificial skin, and big explosions can be done without the use of computers. For example, falling dry foams can be used to display snow in movies or commercials.

1. Keying or compositing is a digital method that combined or mixes two photograms. This effect is accomplished by removing a portion of a photogram, a certain color, usually green or blue, in order to uncover what lies beneath it.
2. Make-up.
3. Gravity's sound effects are recorded underwater.
4. Computer animations.

- Best software for special effect.

1. Adobe Premiere Pro
2. After Effects

- Importance of special effects in filmmaking.

Special effects give freedom to filmmakers, writers and directors to tell any story they like and added creativity to present it to their audience. Special effects are providing both monetary and creative advantages to the studios and filmmakers. They play a very important role, especially today, in not only the movie industry but in television, commercials, and other content.

Chapter 21
Animation Production

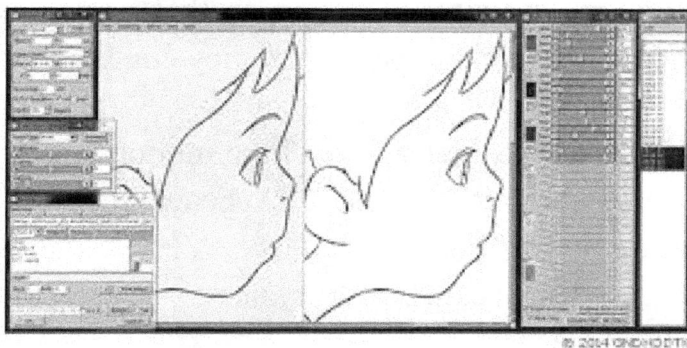

- How is animation produced?

1. Pre-production begins with the main concepts which are initially turned into a full story, and then, once the story has been finalized, other things such as the script, shot sequence, and camera angles are worked on.

2. Story boarding helps finalize the development of the storyline, and is an essential stage of the animation process. It is made up of drawings in the form of a comic strip, and is used to help visualize the animation and to communicate ideas clearly.

Author Dr Boniface Ikejiani

3. Once the story boards have been approved, they are sent to the layout department which then works closely with the director to design the locations and costumes.

4. Model sheets are precisely drawn groups of pictures that show all of the possible expressions that a character can make, and all of the many poses that they could adopt.

5. In order to give a better idea of the motion and timing of complex animation sequences, VFX-heavy scenes, the pre-visualization department within the VFX studio creates simplified mock-ups called "Animatics".

6. When the story board has been approved, the project enters the production phase: layout, modeling, texturing, lighting, rigging and animation.

- Importance of animation production.

In this modern society, the arts are our biggest hope and success for a better world.
1. Simplifies the challenge.
2. Offers an escape.
3. Gives emotional connection.

- Best animation software.

1. Maya
2. Softimage
3. 3D MAX

Author Dr Boniface Ikejiani

Chapter 22
Costuming/Tailoring

- What is costuming?

Costuming is a style of dress, including garments, accessories and hairstyle, especially as a characteristic of a particular country, period or people.

- Functions of a good costumier.

The costume designer collaborates with the director and also responsible to both the producer and director.
The functions of a costume designer includes:

Author Dr Boniface Ikejiani

1. Collaborating with the director on establishing a design for the costumes.
2. Taking measurements of all the cast members.
3. Buys, rents or borrows costumes and accessories.
4. Adapts clothing to suit a character.
5. Sews costumes if necessary.
6. Supplies rehearsal costumes.
7. Attends rehearsals.
8. Coordinates dressers for costume changes.
9. Arranges to repair and clean costumes during the run.

- Qualifications of a good costumier.

A good costumier should have:
1. Strong visual sense.
2. Knowledge of clothing styles and history.
3. Strong interpersonal skills.
4. Strong communication skills.
5. Strong organizational skills.
6. Strong supervisory skills.

- Importance of costuming/tailoring.

Most theater and movie productions are incomplete without the addition of costumes. Costuming plays an important role in the drama, character creation, visual aesthetic and even practical elements in a production.

Author Dr Boniface Ikejiani

Chapter 23
Make-up/Hair artist

- Who is a make-up/hair artist?

A make-up/hair artist is a person whose profession is to use their skills and imagination to transform or enhance the appearance of a person.

Author Dr Boniface Ikejiani

- What are their functions?

Make-up/Hair artist occupy an important place in film making. Their personality type should be creative and adaptable. Their functions are to create make-ups and hairstyles that meet production requirements, and to oversee make-up and hair continuity during filming.

- What are their qualifications?

Qualifications for a make-up/hair artist require little formal education. First of all, a career in one of these fields require patience and imagination. It is perfect for artistic individuals who want to do special effects and prosthetics for film, theater, television or to improve someone's appearance. Most of them completed a cosmetology, or hairdressing programs where they can obtain the skills they'll need.

- Qualities of a good make-up/hair artist.

The most important qualities of a make-up/hair artist are:

1. Trust.
2. Creative imagination.
3. Strong visual sense.
4. Communicative.
5. Confidence and tact.
6. Stamina.

Author Dr Boniface Ikejiani

7. Ability to work under pressure.
8. Methodical.
9. Attentive to details.

Author Dr Boniface Ikejiani

Chapter 24
Line Producing

- What is line producing?

Line producing is a job undertaken by a line producer that is, some kind of a film producer who is the key manager during daily operations of a feature film, advertisement film, television film, or an episode of a TV program. Line producing primarily involves taking care of the logistics of the production from the pre-production stage to the completion of production.

Author Dr Boniface Ikejiani

- How to become a line producer.

Line producers usually come from the ranks of assistant directors and unit production managers, giving them a strong background in the logistics of filmmaking and time management. It is common for them to continue to perform in one of these roles on projects they line produce. Becoming a line producer doesn't necessarily require attending a film school.

- Qualities of a good line producer.

1. Technically proficient.
2. Knows himself.
3. Seeks self-improvement.
4. Understands his team and looks out for them.
5. Keeps his cast and crew informed.
6. Lead by example.
7. Makes sure that the task is understood.
8. Trains his crew to work together.
9. Makes timely decisions.
10. Delegates responsibilities.
11. Challenges his crew.
12. Challenges himself.

Author Dr Boniface Ikejiani

Chapter 25

Catering Services

Although catering may seem insignificant to Nollywood, it is an integral part of the movie industry. While on locations, especially outside a studio, it is important that the actors/actresses and the other crew members are well fed while the shooting lasts.

It is also important that people in the studio are fed too. Acting is a time-consuming and energy-sapping activity that requires everyone on the location to replenish the lost energy during the shooting. This lays the emphasis on the importance of having a good Catering Service on hand to attend to the needs of the huge number of people involved in the movie production.

A brief history of catering

Catering is a business that involves the provision of food and drinks for professionals at work or social events. This may be on a remote site or on-site.

Merchant Marines were the first professionals to coin the term when they employed caterers on their ship back then during the WWII. The caterers were saddled with the responsibility of purchasing the ingredients for the food, prepare the food, and serve both the meals and beverages to sailors and the passengers.

In the US, the industry is considered very young. It was after the World War II that caterers who attended to the military during the war decided to make a living from offering catering services as the economy boomed. The sudden surge in the number of the wealthy created a demand for catering services, and they welcomed the new development with open arms.

Author Dr Boniface Ikejiani

Today, many factors have led to the increase in the number of people offering catering services to professionals around the world. These factors include population increase, technical innovations, a sudden rise in tourism activities, and improvement in transportation. Gradually, catering services have become a household name, an integral part of any professional services and industry, acting and the movie industry inclusive.

There is a branch of catering and services known as the cafeteria. This refers to a catering service where waiting staff table service is either non-existence or has little presence. This can be a restaurant or a food service in a school, a big office building, or a corporation.

Author Dr Boniface Ikejiani

Kitchen tools and equipment

Some tools and equipment are necessities for the catering service. A couple of these that people in the catering industry cannot do without include:

Tongs: You need this tool to pick ingredients when working in the kitchen. A pair of tongs can be tossed, flipped, turned, or scraped.

Flat wooden spatula: This is one of the many multitaskers you will find in a kitchen. The flat wooden spatula can be used for turning food during preparation or for mixing food ingredients when necessary. While the rod spoons and metal spatula have some limitations, the flat wooden spatula is an all-rounder tool.

Author Dr Boniface Ikejiani

Measuring cups: The measuring cups are used for measuring liquids while cooking. Some can also be used for measuring dry ingredients.

Mesh strainer: The mesh strainer can be used in the sink for scrubbing vegetables and washing fruit. A medium mesh strainer can perform many functions in the kitchen. It's perfect for scrubbing, sifting, and straining both wet and dry ingredients.

Author Dr Boniface Ikejiani

Food processor: Food processors are used to make some difficult tasks on food preparation easy. It can be used for processing hard nuts and seeds. They can also be used for grinding garlic and onions.

Quart sauté pan: This is a versatile pan that can be used for warming broth, reheating rice, and melting butter for popcorn making.

Chef's knife: A sharp knife is a necessity in a kitchen. A kitchen is never complete without a sharp knife as it is necessary for cutting and slicing of food items, meat, and vegetables.

Development of food service

The food service industry has metamorphosed from a simple, hospitable gesture some centuries ago to a multimillion-dollar industry. It has experienced immense growth over the years with the creation of new departments and branches in the industry, the influx of investors and stakeholders into the sector, and the surge in population and tourism.

These are some of the outstanding developments that the industry has witnessed in recent years:

• **Hospitality culture:** In the ancient Greece, it was the custom to provide food and lodging for stranded strangers. Today, the food service industry has become an integral part of any establishment. That gesture gradually gave birth to the food industry.

• **Increased population:** Increasing population led to an increased demand for catering services all around the world. This is supported by the advent of new technologies that make food preparation very easy. The food industry is always expected to grow with the increasing population.

• **Fast food centers:** Fast food services are springing up in the major cities of the world, offering catering services to corporations and individuals. With their variety of both local

Author Dr Boniface Ikejiani

and intercontinental dishes, they have become a force to reckon with in the food industry.

- **Automated machine:** Many stakeholders in the industry are putting up vending and automated machines for the sale of food products. Purchases are made with the insertion of the right amount of coins into the vending machine.

- **Introduction of new food products:** With each passing day, the food industry comes up with tons of new food products. These produces are more convenient to prepare than the previous food products. This has led to an astronomical rise the growth of the food industry.

- **Modern food service equipment:** Food preparation has never been this easy. Many people can now have access to food service equipment that helps them in food preparation at the speed of light.

There has been an appreciable growth in the food industry and the trend seems not to be slowing down in the future.

Author Dr Boniface Ikejiani

New trends in food service

The food service industry is growing at an alarming rate with different trends coming up now and then. For instance, the industry has seen these new trends in recent years:

- **Organic foods:** For years, there has been a rapid growth in the organic food industry as many people and corporate bodies are championing the cause of organic foods. Its growth can also be attributed to the increased awareness about the side consequences of genetically-modified and pesticide-treated foods.

- **Anything-free:** People are known with intolerance to some ingredients such as gluten, dairy, or wheat in their food. Recently, the general public is gradually realizing the health benefit of consuming foods that are free of these harmful ingredients. This has led to the thriving of the gluten-free products and other products that are free of all these harmful ingredients.

- **All-natural ingredients:** This is another new and now common trend in the food industry. The health risks associated with foods that are spiced with additives and preservatives has led to the proliferation of the all-natural foods too. While organic foods need government certification to be considered good for consumption, the

Author Dr Boniface Ikejiani

rules and regulations governing the production and sourcing of all-natural foods are a little less restrictive.

• **Alternative protein:** In addition to the two trends mentioned above, another common trend is the shift to vegetarian protein as a means of giving vegetarians access to meatless protein. As the number of vegans increases globally, there is a corresponding increase in the popularity and acceptance of alternative protein sources.

• **Healthy snacks:** Snacking is one of the ways most people keep themselves fueled up while carrying out their day-to-day activities. This has made the healthy snacks sector of the food industry to be growing at an alarming rate. As a result, the snacking frequency of people around the world has increased. The production crew and others involved are not left out of this. Whenever there is the need for fast food, most people on the set will go for healthy snacks.

These are just a few of the common trend in the food service industry. As the industry grows, more new trends are expected to come up in the future.

Skills needed in catering service

Some of the valuable skills needed in the catering service include the following:

Good communication skills: Since you will be coming across many clients from different backgrounds and of different educational status, a professional catering service will have on its board employees with good communication skills. They must be able to converse effectively with actors and actresses from all walks of life.

Dedication: Such an individual must be dedicated to his or her responsibilities. This includes swift response to the clients' requests as well as doing everything possible to ensure clients' satisfaction.

Team spirit: A professional member of a catering service group should be ready to work together with other members of the team. When the principle of division of labor is implemented, each member of the team should be ready to perform his or her assigned tasks.

Personal hygiene: A good personal hygiene is one of the most important qualities expected from the staff of a competent catering service company. A dirty catering service member of staff will be a put off for the clients and customers. This will, without doubt, be bad for business.

Author Dr Boniface Ikejiani

This underscores the importance of the need for people in that line of business to consider their personal hygiene first. It goes a long way in determining people's attitude towards them.

Caterers should keep their hair clean and well combed. Ladies should clip their hair or breaded.

The uniform must be fit, clean, and well-maintained. Sagging is not allowed while shirts must be properly buttoned.

Men should not roll their sleeves. It should be buttoned.

Ability to keep calm under pressure: There may be a huge surge in demand for their services at any time. Depending on the number of people that are engaged in a production, the catering service may have to attend to the numerous needs of scores of people at the same time in a location. This may pose a huge demand and pressure on the catering service.

This calls for the members to have the ability not to lose their cool under pressure. They must learn how to keep going regardless of the huge pressure on them. That will help them attend to the needs of their customers easily without creating an unnecessary friction between them and the crew members. Ability to exercise a high level of professionalism is required to put the situation under control.
Author Dr Boniface Ikejiani

Types of catering services

Catering services come in different forms. The commonest catering services types are:

1. Corporate catering

Corporate catering is a type of catering service that is designed for corporate individuals. It is usually designed for office meetings, training, regional events, and other corporate gatherings. It affords the participants in such meetings to have access to good food on site without leaving the meeting venue. This helps them to save time and money. As a result, they are able to concentrate on the objective of the task that brought them together.

Author Dr Boniface Ikejiani

Other events that are covered by corporate catering include Christmas parties and other holidays that are celebrated in the office.

2. Social event catering

Catering services at retirement and birthday parties are some typical examples of social event catering. It also involves BBQ parties and other social events. Depending on the nature of the event, social events catering involves serving different foods and drinks to guests.

Author Dr Boniface Ikejiani

3. Office catering

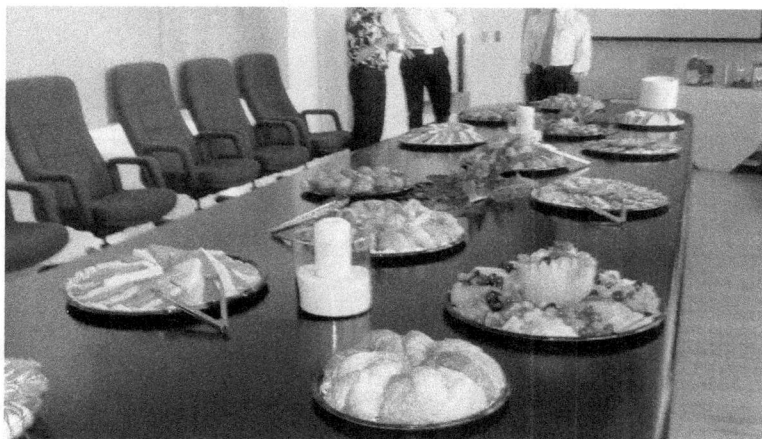

Office catering is gradually becoming one of the most popular catering services in recent years. As more people work for long hours in the office, it is becoming increasingly necessary for caterers to increase the amount of time they spend attending to people at work.

This type of catering service also covers attending to actors and other crew members in the studio or an outdoor location. This ensures that these professionals are able to concentrate on their jobs without having to worry about how and where to get the next meal.

Author Dr Boniface Ikejiani

4. Wedding catering

Weddings are special occasions for people to solemnize their relationship. This has always led to the desire of the couple to invite people to grace that defining moment in their lives.

One of the highlights of a wedding is the reception party. Entertaining the guests at a reception party requires the services of a competent catering service.

Author Dr Boniface Ikejiani

These are some of the types of catering services offered by caterers to meet the growing needs of the increasing number of people who need a catering service for one reason or the other.

Laws, Regulations, and Licenses for Catering Services in Nigeria

Operating a catering service in Nigeria requires that you have the right licenses to operate. The laws and regulations governing businesses in Nigeria demand that you have these licenses:

1. Business Licenses and Permits

To operate any business in Nigeria, you are required to register with the Corporate Affairs Commission (CAC). This body is empowered by the federal government of Nigeria to issue out business licenses and permits to individuals and corporate organizations that meet the basic requirements for registering their businesses.

2. Business Registration

In addition to the licenses and permits, the government also demands that you have a valid business registration license issued by the state government of the state of your residence.

3. Catering license

Since you are not preparing the food in the client's kitchen as a chef, the law demands that you get this license too. The government has establishments that are saddled with the responsibility of ensuring that business owners who meet the basic requirements for licensing are issued this license.

Dos and Don'ts of catering service

Catering is not all about being an expert in your chosen field only. It also includes having a good customer service. There are many do's and don'ts you must practice to boost your reputation as a good caterer. Here are some of these rules:

• **Do what you are good at:** While you may be trained in different culinary delicacies, there are chances that you are very good in a particular area. This may be in pastries, desserts, or soul food. While trying to be a Jack of all trades will bring out the best in you, specializing in what you are good at will have a lasting benefit. You should try all you can to stay focused on your strength rather than being tempted to dabble into what will bring you down.

• **Be fair with your pricing:** One of the most important factors that your potential clients will want to consider before hiring you is your pricing. This requires that you do whatever you can to make your pricing to be reasonable while trying to get credit for your expertise.

The two factors you should always put in mind when pricing are the reality of stiff competition and the budget of your client. Making every effort to know the pricing of your competitors and your client's budget will make it possible for you to arrive at a balance when pricing.

If your pricing is fair, your clients will be more than ready to transact business with you.

- **Don't stress yourself out:** It is a common knowledge that the catering service itself is very challenging. Yet, your success as a caterer depends on your ability to effectively manage stress. If you stress yourself out while rendering service to your client, this may have a negative impact on your service. If that happens, your clients may be stressed out as well. The result will be catastrophic.

- **Don't ignore your customers' wants:** You may have an unquestionable expertise that makes you have absolute confidence in your approach towards the task at hand while providing service for your clients. Nevertheless, always remember to consider their opinions. Customers are always right and if there is a deviation from what they want, it may endanger your already built reputation.

Author Dr Boniface Ikejiani

- **Don't interrupt your client while talking:** It is consider a rude behavior to interrupt your client when communicating with you. You must listen attentively and wait patiently to add your input or respond until it is your turn to do so. It is accorded a sign of respect for your client. It is also regarded as a display of professionalism.

- **Do know your menu:** A competent caterer knows his or her menu so that customers' orders can be swiftly attended to. You should leverage on your knowledge efficiently when dealing with your guest. This is regarded as one of the ways to win their hearts. However, don't use your knowledge to show off. This will in turn have a negative impact on your brand.

- **Don't chat at work:** Spending your time communicating with your coworkers or being active on the phone while you were supposed to attend to your clients is a big no. Your clients won't appreciate such attitude.

- **Do replace cups:** If your client is already using a cup to drink water, don't use the same cup to serve him wine if he requests for wine. You should replace the cup immediately.

Consumer goodwill and food service ethics

When relating to the client, a caterer must display some important service ethics. This ranges from their dressing and grooming to communication technique.
Some important ethics include:

- **The caterer must speak with clarity:** He or she must ensure that the client understands the message he is passing across. Ability to clearly present your message is one of the many ways to impress your client.

- **The caterer must speak audibly:** A good conversational quality involves speaking audibly enough for the clients to hear you without straining their ears.

- **Be courteous:** Your clients must be treated with respect. Courtesy demands that you appreciate their good suggestions while you apologize whenever you are at fault. Some expressions such as May I, Please, I'm sorry, and other related expressions are a sign of courtesy that your clients will appreciate.

- **Stay away from unpleasant habits:** Your clients won't take you seriously if you display some detestable attitude such as smoking, spitting, yawning, handling their food with bare hands, and other unpleasant habits. Avoid these bad habits while attending to clients.
Author Dr Boniface Ikejiani

Cultivating the right etiquette will go a long way in helping you to have a good relationship with your clients.

The seven rules of catering service

These seven rules are generally considered as the rule of thumb for any caterer that is considered to be a professional.

Whether when providing a private or general service, the following rules should be strictly adhered to:

Author Dr Boniface Ikejiani

Rule 1: Serve women before men

When you are faced with serving men and women, the former should be served first, followed by the former. The only exception to this is when they are in the company of children. In this case, the children should be served first, followed by the women, and finally, the men.

Rule 2: Serve food from the left side of the guests

When serving a couple of guests, perhaps in a table, you should commence your service from the left side of the table. The goal is to avoid putting you in a tight and awkward position. This requires that the serving should be done in the clockwise position.

Rule 3: Serve beverages from the guests' right

Since the majority of the guests are right-handed, it is logical that you start serving the drinks from their right hands. If there are left-handed guests, adapt your serving to take care of that. You should place alcoholic beverages on a cocktail napkin in front of your guest. If you want to serve water, it is best to serve it with your right hand while you fold your left hand behind your back.

Author Dr Boniface Ikejiani

Rule 4: Bring all the foods at the same time

If there is an order from a table, it is a good practice to bring all the foods at once. It is the manager's responsibility to make sure that the guests are served simultaneously.

Rule 5: Remove dirty plates only when the guests are done with eating

You should give your guest the highest regard. It speaks well of you if you wait until all the guests have finished eating before clearing the table.

Rule 6: Don't stack or scrape dirty dishes on your guest's table

It is a sign of disrespect if you scrape dirty dishes on your guest's table. You should desist from this act.

Rule 7: Dirty dishes removal should be done from your guest's right side

This rule stipulates that you remove all the dishes by first removing any dirty silverware with your right hand. Transfer it to your left and follow a similar routine when removing the plate too. You should do this in the clockwise direction.

As a catering service provider, you must acquaint yourself with these rules and make the best use of them.

Generally, the issues discussed in this chapter will be helpful when dealing with your clients. Applying them increases your chances of satisfying your clients, a recipe for career success.

Author Dr Boniface Ikejiani

Chapter 26
Property management

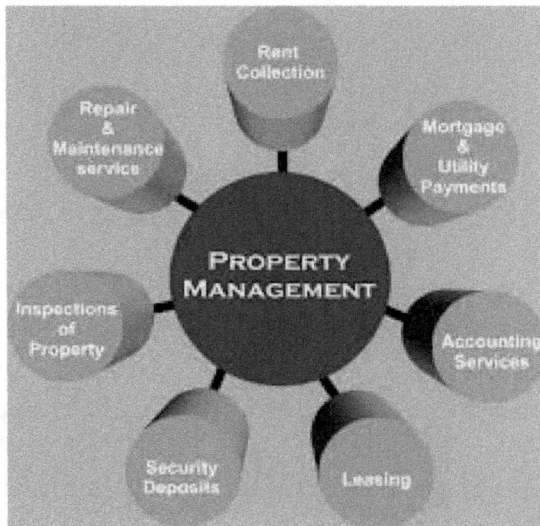

- What is property management?

Property management is the operation, control, and oversight of real estate as used in its most broad terms. Management indicates a need to be cared for, monitored and accountability is given for its useful life and condition.

- Why is property management needed in Nollywood?

1. The most important benefit of property management to owners of houses for rent and other real estate properties is the preservation of their properties;
2. Collecting rents is one of the primary duties of a property manager. It involves the timely collection of rents and book-keeping services like payment of bills and mortgage payments if requested;
3. Taking care of regular maintenance and repairs of the property. Once you accept paying tenants, you are expected to resolve maintenance issues promptly;
4. Providing security to the property, the property manager is also responsible for securing the premises of the property from thefts, fires, illegal intrusions and other man-made hazards.

- What makes a good property manager?

A property manager must know how to juggle many tasks, keeping both owners and tenants satisfied. Qualities that a property manager should possess include:
1. Education and experience.
2. People skills.
3. Organizational qualities.
4. Detail-oriented.

Author Dr Boniface Ikejiani

Chapter 27
Production management

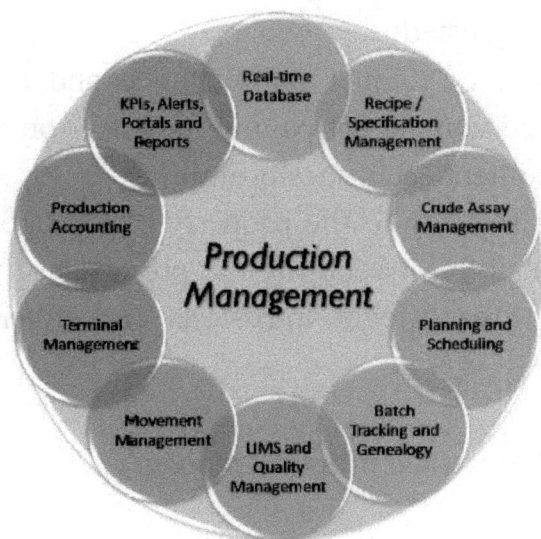

- What is production management?

Production management involves controlling and coordinating the activities required to make a product, typically involving effective control of scheduling, cost, performance, quality, and waste requirements.

Author Dr Boniface Ikejiani

- What are the functions of a production manager?

The production manager's responsibilities and functions are "people management," choosing the machines and methods that will be used in the realization of the product or service, the management of flow processes such as raw materials and paperwork and the concern for money explained by the importance of financing and asset utilization to most organizations.

- Scope of production management in movie making.

1. Location of facilities.
2. Product design.
3. Production and planning control.
4. Quality control.
5. Materials management.
6. Maintenance management.

- Qualities of a good production manager.

Being a manager involves a lot of work and patience. What makes a good production manager? The qualities are:
1. Strategic thinker.
2. Passion for the product.
3. Empathizes with the customer.
4. Interviews customers.
5. Aspires to build great user experience.
Author Dr Boniface Ikejiani

6. Keeps score.
7. Ability to prioritize.
8. Collaborative leader.
9. Execution.

Author Dr Boniface Ikejiani

Chapter 28
Production designing

- What is production designing?

Production designing is responsible for the overall visual look of the production. It involves selection of settings and style to visually relate the story.

- How to become a production designer.

A production designer is first of all a creative personality type.

Author Dr Boniface Ikejiani

To become a production designer you need to be a creative. First of all, you need to be a graduate of art (architecture, theatre, interior or 3D design courses). After that, you can then complete a specialist course in film or theatre design.

- The importance of production designing in filmmaking.

Production designing has a key role in the creation of movies and television. As a production designer, you will have to work directly with the director, cinematographer and the producer to select the way the story will be visually felt.

- What makes a good production designer?

A good production designer has a handful of qualities, such as:
1. Design skills.
2. Knowledge of art.
3. Skilled in computer software.
4. Ability to inspire and motivate a team.
5. Show of excellent management skills.
6. Good communication and presentation skills.
7. Tactical.

Author Dr Boniface Ikejiani

Chapter 29
Movie Funding

- How are movies funded?

Film finance is an aspect of film production that occurs during the development stage prior to pre-production, and is concerned with determining the potential value of a proposed film.

Film finance is a subset of project finance, meaning the film's project generated cash flows rather than external sources are used to repay investors. The main factors determining the commercial success of a film include public taste, artistic merit, competition from other films released at

Author Dr Boniface Ikejiani

the same time, the quality of the script, the quality of the cast, the quality of the director and other parties. Even if a film looks like it will be a commercial success, there is still no accurate method of determining the levels of revenue the film will generate.

- How to get funding for your movie.

1. Equity
2. Pre-Sales
3. Gap
4. Tax Incentives
5. Deferred and crowdfunding
6. Private equity

Chapter 30
Equipment Leasing/Studio service provider

- How are equipment leased?

1. Capital Lease: In a capital lease, your business receives all benefits and drawbacks of owning the equipment. All assets and liabilities of the equipment are placed on your business's balance sheet used for equipment you plan to purchase at the end of the lease period. Examples of capital leases include the $1 buyout lease and 10% option lease.

2. Operating Lease: An operating lease leaves equipment off your balance sheet. On paper, your lender owns the equipment and gets to take advantage of any depreciation. Typically best when financing equipment with a short shelf life, or equipment you plan on replacing at the end of the

lease. An example of an operating lease is a fair market value lease.

- The best studio service providers in Hollywood.

Universal Studios

Chapter 31
Video Rentals

- Top video rentals.

1. Spiderman: Homecoming
2. Wonder Woman
3. War for the Planet of the Apes
4. Baby Driver
5. Atomic Blonde

Author Dr Boniface Ikejiani

- Impact of video renting on Hollywood.

Video sales and rentals opened a new mass market in the entertainment industry—the home movie viewer—and offered Hollywood an extended source of income from its films.

Author Dr Boniface Ikejiani

Chapter 32
Marketing/Distribution

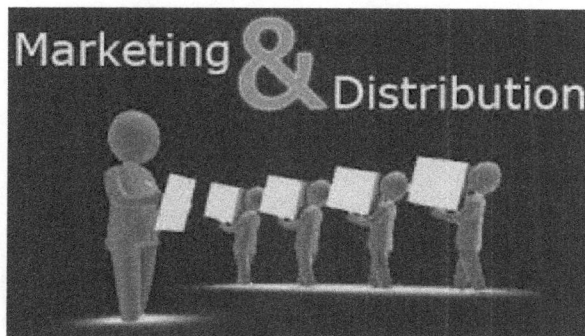

- Importance of marketing and distributing movies.

Film marketing plays an important role in increasing the revenue of film production company. The advantage of good publicity is that even if the movie fails to meet the audience's standards, with enough curious ticket or other media buyers, the Film Making Company can regain its money spent on the campaign, or even gain some profit out of it if they are lucky enough.

Author Dr Boniface Ikejiani

- Best marketing/distributing strategies.

1. Deadpool – iconic poster.
2. The Secret Life of Pets – a marketing campaign that targeted pet lovers of all ages, versus just focusing on families and also blanketed theaters with trailers.
3. Suicide Squad – the soundtrack.
4. This is Us – advertising on social media.
5. Publicity stunt.
6. IMDB reviews.
7. Video advertising.
8. Viral marketing campaign, involving the audience.
9. Interactive Facebook Page (games, contests, apps).
10. Use niche social networks – vine, Instagram, Pinterest.
11. Personal Marketing.
12. Google AdWords.

- Best marketing/distributing companies in Hollywood.

1. Paramount Pictures
2. 20th Century Fox
3. Lowes
4. Universal Studios
5. Warner Bros
6. Columbia Pictures
7. United Artists
8. RKO Pictures

Author Dr Boniface Ikejiani

Chapter 33
Exhibition

- What is movie exhibition?

Exhibition is the retail branch of the film industry. It involves not the production or the distribution of motion pictures, but their public screening, usually for paying customers in a site devoted to such screenings, the movie theater. What the exhibitor sells is the experience of a film (and frequently, concessions like soft drinks and popcorn). Because exhibitors to some extent control how films are programmed, promoted, and presented to the

Author Dr Boniface Ikejiani

public, they have considerable influence over the box-office success, and more importantly, the reception of films.

- Types of exhibition.

1. Cinema – the distributor is paid by the cinema for a copy of the film.

2. Home – the distributor is paid by the company who is selling the film for a copy.

- Importance of exhibition.

Digital exhibition is important for film industry because it means that non-mainstream films are becoming more accessible. Independent cinemas have the capability to screen more films because digital distribution and exhibition is cheaper than traditional methods.

Chapter 34
Painting Sculptures

- The roles of art in the movies.

Art in the movies is responsible for arranging the overall look of the film. Art is a very important part of our education, and since almost everyone is watching movies, art may develop some emotions and feeling in the audience.

Author Dr Boniface Ikejiani

- Artwork used in movies.

1. "Time out to be within" was used in "Surrogates"

2. "Bound" was used in "Surrogates"

Author Dr Boniface Ikejiani

3. "Paradox" was used in "Surrogates"

4. "Abstraction in Red and Green, 1958" was used in "Surrogates"

Author Dr Boniface Ikejiani

5. "Red Suit" was used in "Surrogates"

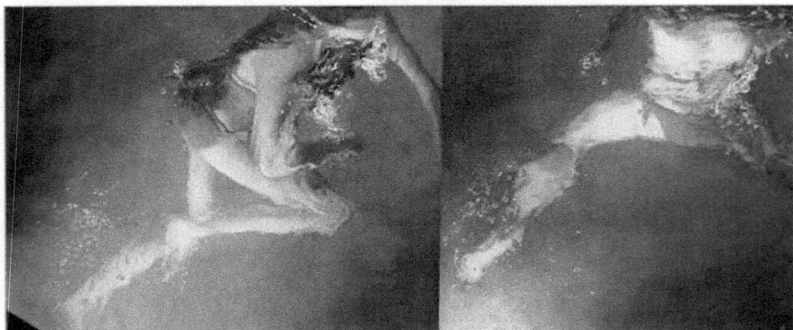

6. "Moist Lowlands" was used in "The Company Men"

Author Dr Boniface Ikejiani

7. "Tenderly" was used in "The Company Men"

8. "Imperial Ballet" was used in "The Company Men"

Author Dr Boniface Ikejiani

9. "Mort Bleu II" was used in "The Company Men"

10. "Grand Odalisque" was used in "The Company Men"

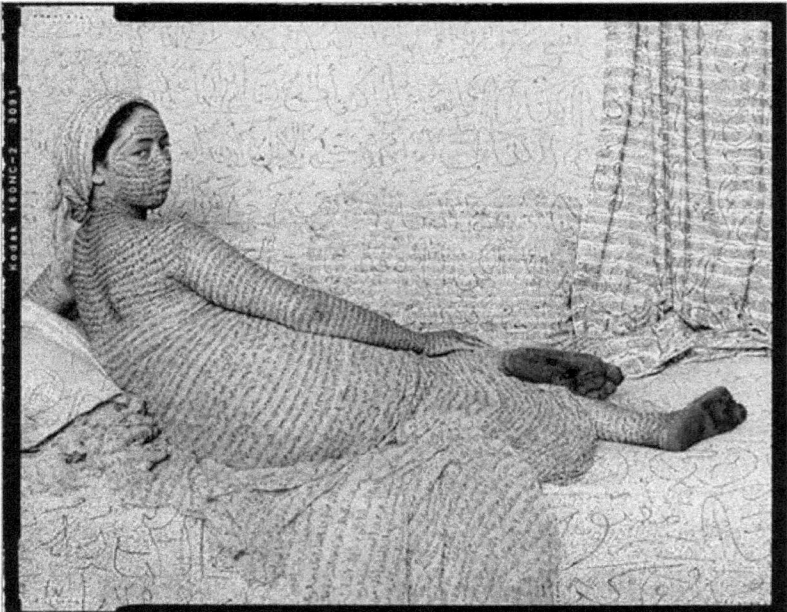

Author Dr Boniface Ikejiani

11. "Ship Hull No. 15" was used in "The Company Men"

12. "Blue Blood" was used in "The Women"

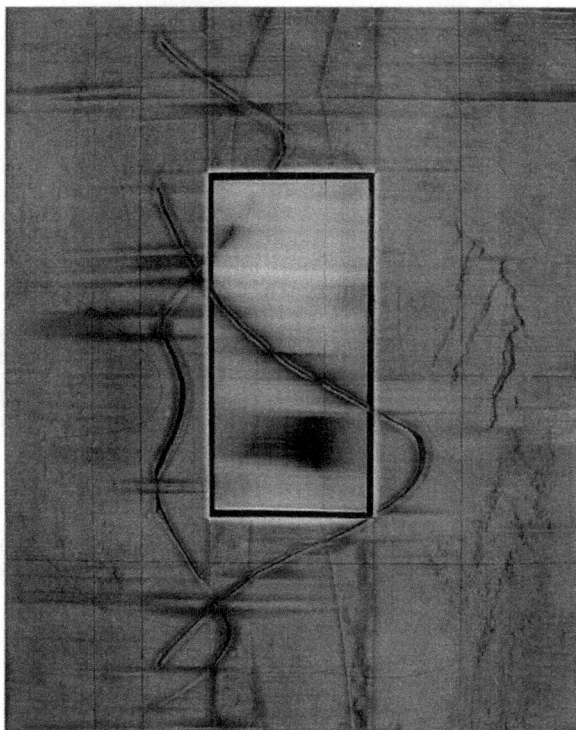

Author Dr Boniface Ikejiani

13. "Guilin" was used in "The Town"

14. "The Starry Night" was used in "I am Legend"

15. "Saturn Devouring his Children" was used in "Wall Street: Money Never Sleeps"

16. "Post-Dogmatist Paining #326" was used in "Twilight Saga: Breaking Dawn 1"

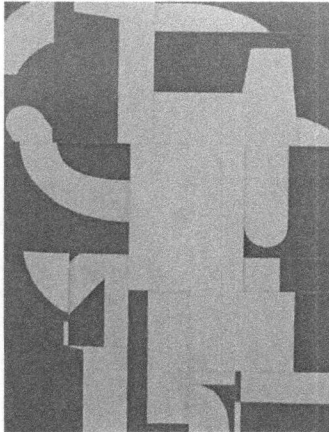

Author Dr Boniface Ikejiani

17. "The Lonely Maiden" was used in "The Maiden Heist"

18. "Jeanne Samary in a Low Necked Dress" was used in "La migliore offerta"

Author Dr Boniface Ikejiani

19. "Seine at Argenteuil" was used in "Vanilla Sky"

20. "Road with Cypress and Star" was used in "A good year"

Author Dr Boniface Ikejiani

21. "Luncheon of the Boating Party" was used in "Amelie"

22. "The Mirror of Venus" was used in "The Thomas Crown Affair"

Author Dr Boniface Ikejiani

23. "The Fighting Temeraire" was used in "Skyfall"

24. "The Political Lady" was used in "The Age of Innocence"

Author Dr Boniface Ikejiani

25. "Water Lilies" was used in "Titanic"

26. "The Young Ladies of Avignon" was used in "Titanic"

Author Dr Boniface Ikejiani

27. "Woman with a Fan" was used in "Skyfall"

28. "La Mariée" was used in "Notting Hill"

Author Dr Boniface Ikejiani

29. "View from Kitchen - Sunset" was used in "Eyes Wide Shut"

30. "Certain Uncertainties" was used in "The Thomas Crown Affair"

Author Dr Boniface Ikejiani

31. "Puberty" was used in "V for Vendetta"

32. "Ex nihilo recreation" was used in "The Devil's Advocate"

Author Dr Boniface Ikejiani

33. "Bather" was used in "Midnight in Paris"

34. "The Duel after the Masquerade" was used in "The Age of Innocence"

Author Dr Boniface Ikejiani

35. "Ochre and Red on Red" was used in "Iron Man 3"

36. "Number 1 Lavender Mist" was used in "Mona Lisa Smile"

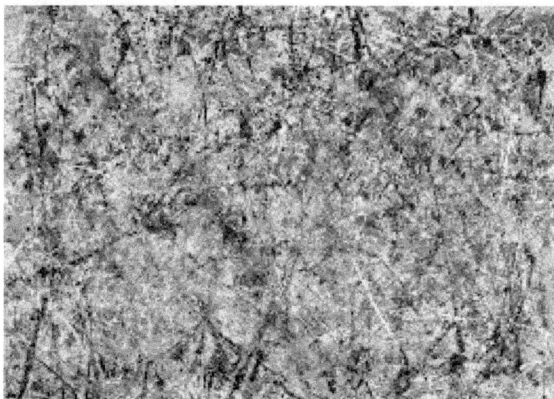

Author Dr Boniface Ikejiani

37. "The Sleeping Gypsy" was used in "I am Legend"

38. "Figure with Meat" was used in "Batman"

Author Dr Boniface Ikejiani

39. "Bear" was used in "Amelie"

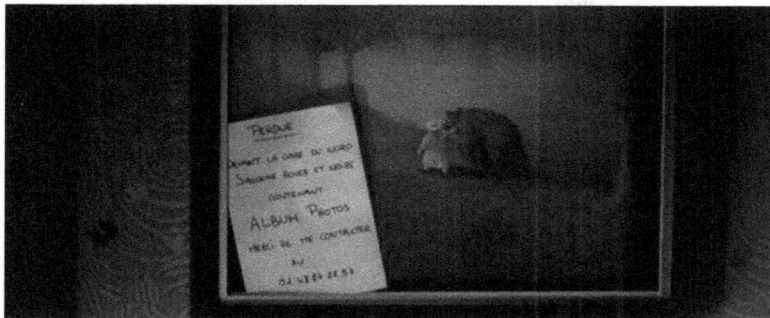

40. "Guernica" was used in ""Children of Men"

Author Dr Boniface Ikejiani

41. "The Kiss (Lovers)" was used in "Dying Young"

42. "Harbor #3" was used in "The Devil Wears Prada"

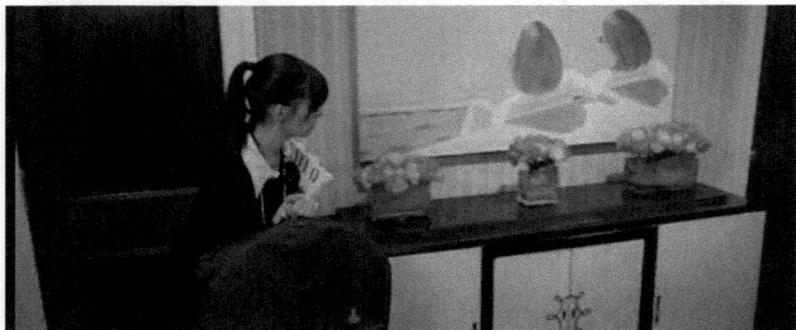

Author Dr Boniface Ikejiani

43. "Death and the Miser" was used in "In Bruges"

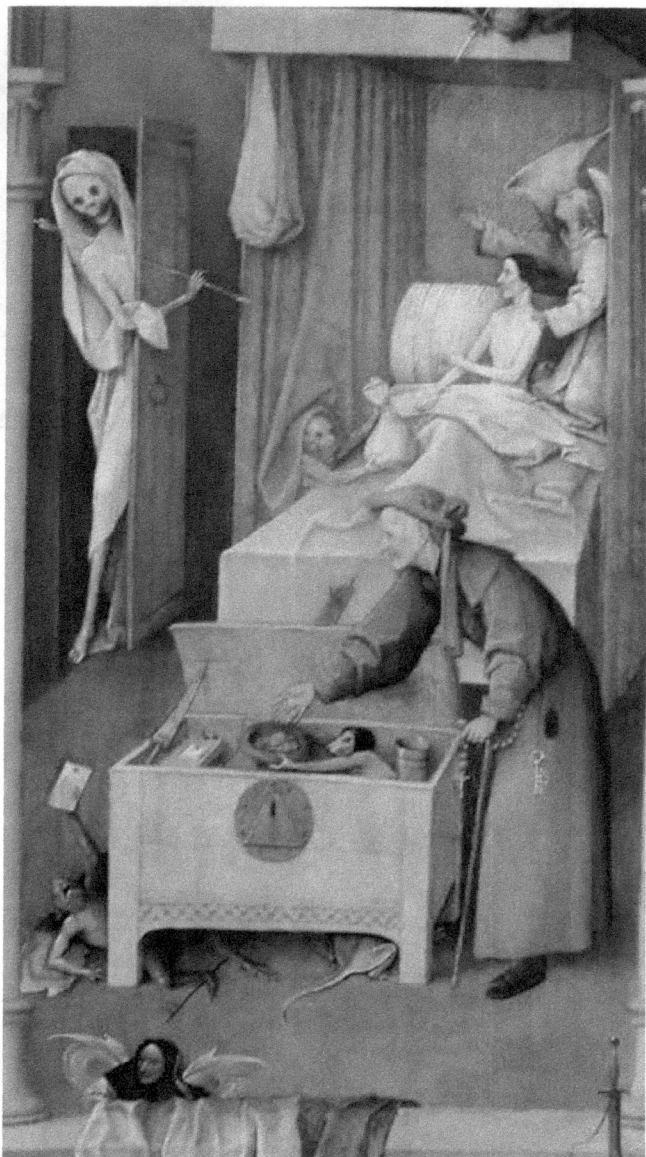

Author Dr Boniface Ikejiani

44. "The Garden of Earthly Delights" was used in "What Dreams May Come"

45. "Paysage" was used in "Wall Street"

Author Dr Boniface Ikejiani

46. "Venting Cattle on the Frisco System" was used in "Giant"

47. "Men in the Cities" was used in "American Psycho"

Author Dr Boniface Ikejiani

48. "Portrait of Mia" was used in "Pulp Fiction"

49. "Swim Party" was used in "Something's Gotta Give"

Author Dr Boniface Ikejiani

50. "Head of Demon" was used in "The Vampire Chronicles"

51. "Three Musicians" was used in "Entrapment"

52. "Two Seats" was used in "Something's Gotta Give"

Author Dr Boniface Ikejiani

53. "Girl with Lantern" was used in "Message in a Bottle"

Author Dr Boniface Ikejiani

54. "The Biglin Brothers Racing" was used in "House of Cards"

55. "Last Judgement" was used in "In Bruges"

Author Dr Boniface Ikejiani

Chapter 35
Printing Posters and Jackets

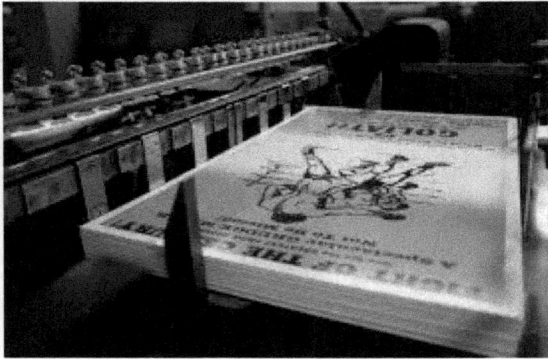

- How to print posters and jackets.

Printing jackets:
1. Print on a good quality jacket.
2. A good hold-down is essential.
3. Use a proven ink system.

Author Dr Boniface Ikejiani

4. Get the ink the proper viscosity.
5. Use the correct screen.
6. A flash cure unit is a must.
7. Print with technique.
8. Auto flash units improve multi-color.
9. Give them a few days to age.
10. Train hard.

Printing posters:
1. Choose a picture.
2. Choose the software tool.
3. Prepare the poster.
4. Print the poster sheets.
5. Crop the margins.
6. Glue the sheets.

- The cost of printing posters and jackets for movies.

The cost of printing posters and jackets varies and depends on how large and how complicated the image is.

- Best posters and jackets printing companies.

1. Jakprints Inc.
2. Awesome Merchandise
3. Threadbird
4. ForHIM

Author Dr Boniface Ikejiani

Chapter 36
DVD/VCD Replication

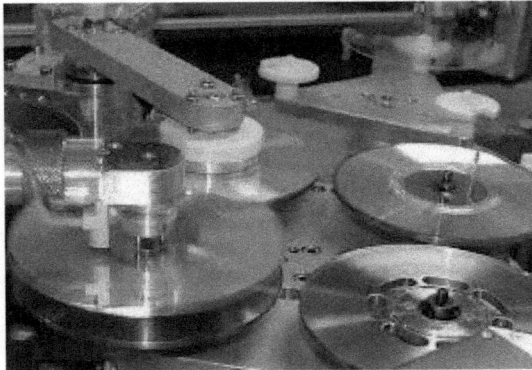

- How are DVDs/VCDs replicated?

DVD/VCD replication is a physical production process that involves actually pressing the discs during manufacture from a glass master (glass that has been coated by a chemical, which is burned off with a laser).

- The cost of replication.

DVD/VCD replication is a very quick and cost-effective production method for larger quantities of discs. Due to the high setup costs, this type of production is not suitable for smaller production runs.

Author Dr Boniface Ikejiani

- Best DVD replication services.

1. Disc Factory
2. Oasis CD
3. Disc Makers
4. Arcube
5. Hellman Production

Chapter 37
Movie Reporting

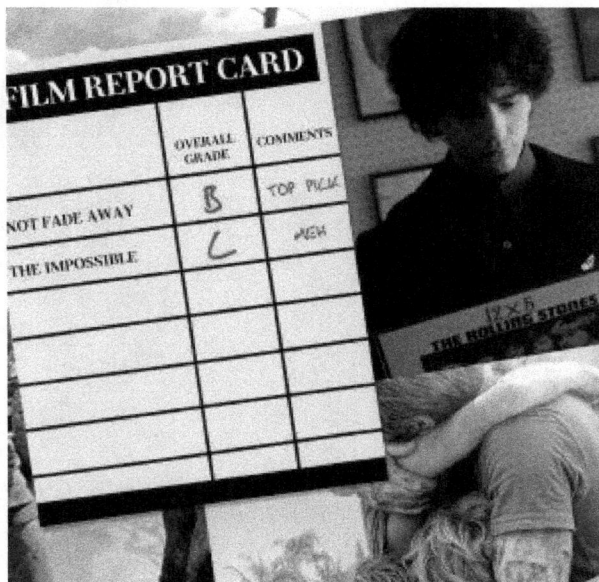

- What is movie reporting?

A movie report is always confused with a movie review, but they are not the same. A movie report has some steps to follow:

1. Attention to themes, things that stand out, colors or music.

2. Take notes.

Author Dr Boniface Ikejiani

3. See the connection of those things.
4. Understanding the context of the character.
5. Develop the thesis statement.
6. Use reasons to support arguments.
7. Show how the film fits society.

- How are movies reported?

Reporting movies takes skill, practice and experience. To be written, a movie report requires the ability to quickly discuss the plot, quality of the acting and other basic details, while also discussing background information like editing and direction.

- Importance of movie reporting.

First of all, in a movie report you need to be very honest because it is very important to the audience. After the written report has being read by the audience, they will choose whether or not to watch that movie and automatically their decisions will affect the ratings of the movie. This may either increase or decrease.

A movie report is also important because they will offer a "trailer" of the story to the audience and it has to stick close to the truth.

Author Dr Boniface Ikejiani

Chapter 38
Training/Capacity Building

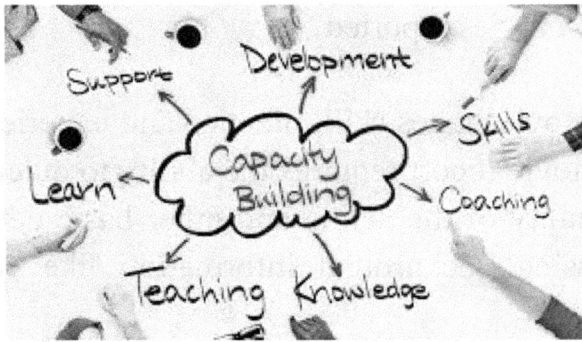

- What is capacity building?

Capacity building (or capacity development) is the process by which individual and organizations obtain, improve, and retain the skills and knowledge needed to do their jobs competently. Capacity building and capacity development are often used interchangeably; however, some people interpret capacity building as not recognizing people's existing capacity whereas capacity development recognizes existing capacities which require improvement.

Author Dr Boniface Ikejiani

- The roles of training/capacity building in Nollywood.

Training/capacity building in Nollywood – film industry – is as important as in any other business.

Capacity building is very important in the film industry because the more a person trains, the more he understands and acknowledges. For instance, actors need the capacity building so as to enter the character's skin much better and will automatically play much better.

Capacity building is very important for the crew also because the crew has an integral role to play as well.

Author Dr Boniface Ikejiani

Chapter 39
Set Designing

- What is set designing?

Set designing represents all the scenery, furniture and props the audience sees at a production of a play.

- Importance of set designing.

Set designing's aim is to "wow" the audience. The bigger the wow factor, the more attention the show attracts and therefore, the ratings.

Author Dr Boniface Ikejiani

- What are the roles of a set designer?

The set designer will normally read the script many times, both to get a feel for the flavor and spirit of the script and to list its specific requirements for scenery, furnishings and props. The time of day, location, season, historical period and any set changes called for in the script are noted. The set designer's focus here is on figuring out everything that may be needed based on the dialogue in the script. Stage directions tend to be ignored at this point in the process.

- Famous set designer.

Ken Adam

Chapter 40
Set Construction

- What is set construction?

Set construction is the process undertaken by a construction manager to build full-scale scenery, as specified by a production designer or art director working in collaboration with the director of a production to create a set for a theatrical, film or television production. The set designer produces a scale model, scale drawings, paint elevations (a scale painting supplied to the scenic painter of each element that requires painting), and research about props, textures, and so on.

Author Dr Boniface Ikejiani

- Set construction techniques.

Set design is one of the unsung arts of movie making. Do it wrong and the audience is sure to think the movie is cheap and has a low budget, Do it right, and most people won't notice at all. This is the point – the best sets aren't flashy or expensive, they simply fit naturally into the scene.

1. Planning your set

a. Study the script.
b. Ask the director about plans, themes or necessary props he/she wants to be incorporated.
c. Sketch a mock-up of the set design.
d. Decide if you're going to build the set or use an existing location.
e. Draft a budget for your set design.

2. Set designing

a. Go location scouting.
b. Discuss what parts of the room you want to use.
c. Think of the room's "lines" when designing.
d. Build, design or buy essential crafts and props.
e. Less is more.
f. Remove or cover up any brand images.
g. Light the set with the cinematographer.

Author Dr Boniface Ikejiani

3. Building flats (fake walls for original sets)

a. Build "flats" to make fake walls for any movie set.

b. Lay your Masonite on the ground to measure out the frame.

c. Place two of your 3x8 wood pieces along the long side of the wood.

d. Measure the distance between the two long pieces of the wood.

e. Lay your cut planks along the top and bottom edge of the Masonite.

f. Hammer your frame together using 1.5" nails.

g. Apply wood glue to the entire frame and press the Masonite onto it.

h. Nail the entire Masonite Board into the frame.

i. Attach your final 3x8 piece of wood into the back of the frame, onto the center.

j. Cut your plywood in half diagonally.

k. Cut a one-foot notch in the center of your plywood's hypotenuse.

l. Use a power drill to screw the plywood into the frame.

m. Use the flats to create the walls of your set, then begin decorating.

• Functions of set construction.

The filmmaker's goal is to make the audience believe in the fictional world he has created. The world could be very

Author Dr Boniface Ikejiani

much like our own or an imaginative fantasy land. But all of the elements of that world - from the buildings to the cars to the contents of the main character's refrigerator - need to work together to tell a story.

Author Dr Boniface Ikejiani

Chapter 41
Carpentry

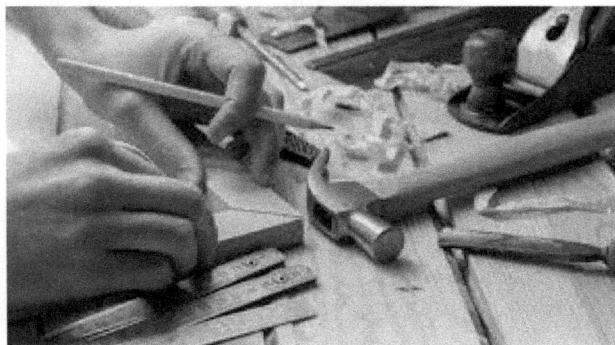

- Why is carpentry needed in filmmaking?

Carpentry is a skilled trade in which the primary work performed is the cutting, shaping and installation of building materials during the construction of buildings, ships, timber bridges, concrete formwork, etc.
Carpentry is needed in filmmaking to help at the set construction.

- The key skills of a carpenter.

1. Mechanical skills
2. Math skills

Author Dr Boniface Ikejiani

3. Detail oriented
4. Critical thinking skills
5. Physical strength
6. Communication

Author Dr Boniface Ikejiani

Chapter 42
Story Sales

3 STEPS TO TELL A POWERFUL SALES STORY

The most powerful way to persuade anyone to do anything, without pressuring them, is to fuel their imagination with an engaging story.

- What is story sales?

In selling techniques, a sales presentation or a sales pitch is a line of talk that attempts to persuade someone or something with a planned sales presentation strategy of a product or service designed to initiate and close a sale of the product or service.

A sales pitch is essentially designed to be either an introduction of a product or service to an audience who knows nothing about it, or a descriptive expansion of a product or service that an audience has already expressed interest in. Sales professionals prepare and give a sales pitch, which can either be formal or informal, and might be delivered in different ways.

- How to make the best story sales?

1. Appeal to both logic and emotion by combining facts with narrative.
2. Use metaphors because metaphors work on the subconscious mind.
3. Always keep it relevant.

- The attributes of a compelling sales story.

1. Connect
2. Challenge
3. Conflict
4. Conquer
5. Conclude

Chapter 43
Poster Pasting

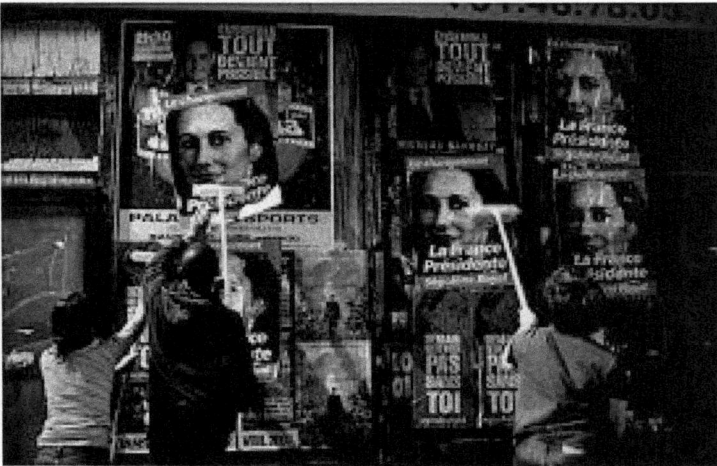

- Why are posters pasted?

A typical poster includes both textual and graphic elements, although a poster may be either wholly graphical or wholly text. Posters are designed to be both eye-catching and informative. They are used frequently as a tool of advertising or as a form of art.

Author Dr Boniface Ikejiani

- Importance of poster pasting to the movie industry.

Movie posters are an important element in the film marketing mix for big film studios and independent productions. They are used as a promotional material, and it encompasses the message and feeling of the film, and it will be the main source of attention for people wanting to read about that movie.

Any article leading up to the release of a movie will have to be able to pinpoint the poster as a reference to the subject matter. It is very important that the artwork behind the poster be at its best to convey the subtlety of the movie, its characters, and its genre.

Author Dr Boniface Ikejiani

Chapter 44
Artist Management

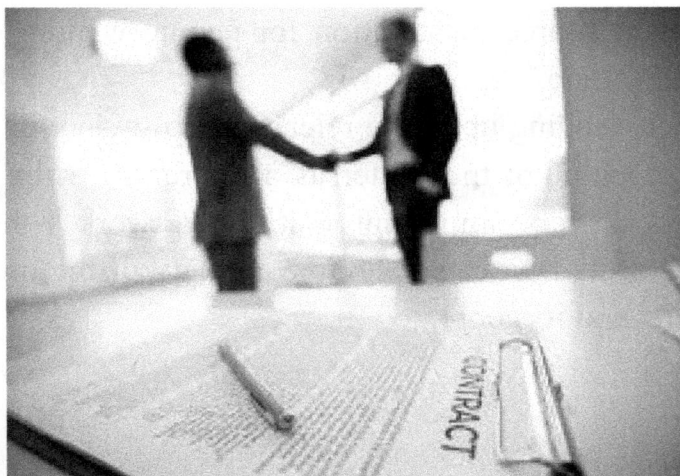

- Who is an artist manager?

An artist manager also known as a talent manager, brand manager or music manager, is an individual or company that guides the professional career of artists in the entertainment industry.

His responsibility is to oversee the day-to-day business affairs of an artist, advice and counsel the talent concerning professional matters, long-term plans and personal decisions which may affect their career.

Author Dr Boniface Ikejiani

- How are artists managed?

An artist manager has to counsel the artist regarding his professional matters, long-term plans and personal decisions. They offer help in finding artists an agent.

Most of artist managers are employed to establish and maintain connections with booking agents, promote the activities of the artist and manage finances in order to optimize the artist's ability to book gigs, establish a fan base and ultimately bring in revenue from their work.

- Qualities of a competent artist manager.

1. Great communicator.
2. Business savvy.
3. Consistently involved.
4. Not a control freak.
5. Passionate about music.

Author Dr Boniface Ikejiani

Chapter 45
Promotion

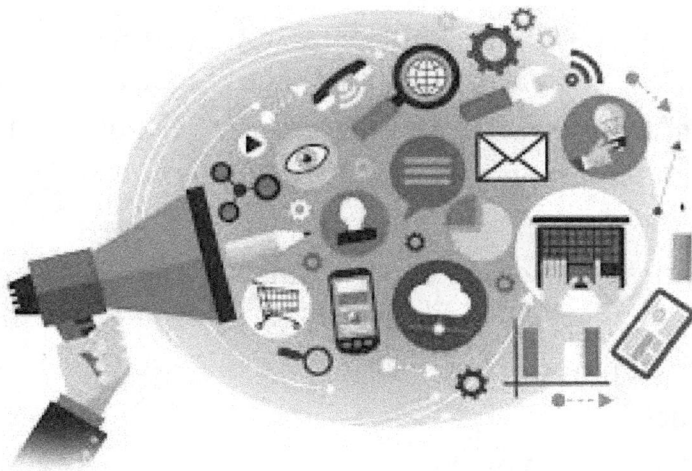

- How are movies promoted?

Film promotion is the practice of promotion specifically in the film industry and usually occurs in coordination with the process of film distribution.

Sometimes called the press junket or film junket, film promotion generally includes press releases, advertising campaigns, merchandising, franchising, media, and interviews with key people involved in the making of the film.

Author Dr Boniface Ikejiani

- Importance of movie promotion.

Movie promotion is about creating awareness. Once awareness is created, then you can build hype and create excitement.
Movie promotion is important for the audience because they will know what to expect from the movie.

- Best promotion techniques.

The best promotion techniques are made in:
1. Theaters
a. Trailers
b. Film posters
c. Slideshows
d. Standees
e. Cardboard 3D displays

2. Television and radio
a. Commercials
b. Newspaper ads
c. On-set posters
d. Action figures
e. Television talk shows
f. Entertainment news programs
g. Advance trailers

Author Dr Boniface Ikejiani

3. Internet
a. Online digital film screens
b. Viral marketing
c. Internet marketing campaign using paid advertisement and social media marketing

4. Print
a. Newspapers, magazines, and inserts in books
b. Cross-promotion of original book
c. Comic special editions or special episodes

5. Merchandising
a. Paid co-branding or co-advertising.
b. Promotional giveaways (branded drink cups, toys, food combinations, etc.)

6. Promotional tours and interviews

7. Audience research

- Best promotion companies.

1. Promo direct
2. rushIMPRINT
3. 4Imprint
4. ePromos
5. Quality Logo Products

Author Dr Boniface Ikejiani

Chapter 46
Insurance Cover for Artist

- How are artistes insured?

Insurance is a means of protection from financial loss. It is a form of risk management primarily used to hedge against the risk of a contingent, and uncertain loss.

An entity which provides insurance is known as an insurer, insurance company, or insurance carrier. A person or entity who buys insurance is known as an insured or policyholder.

Author Dr Boniface Ikejiani

The insurance transaction involves the insured assuming a guaranteed and known relatively small loss in the form of payment to the insurer in exchange for the insurer's promise to compensate the insured in the event of a covered loss. The loss may or may not be financial, but it must be reducible to financial terms, and must involve something in which the insured has an insurable interest established by ownership, possession, or preexisting relationship.

- The importance of providing insurance cover for artistes.

Insurance has evolved as a process of safeguarding the interest of people from loss and uncertainty. It may be described as a social device to reduce or eliminate the risk of loss to life and property.

It is important because:

1. It provides safety and security.

2. It generates financial resources.

3. Life insurance encourages savings.

4. Promotes economic growth.

5. It provides medical support.

Author Dr Boniface Ikejiani

6. Spreading of risk.

7. Source of collecting funds.

• Best insurance companies for artistes.

1. Adrian Flux
2. Mandy
3. Auto Insurance
4. Nippon Life Insurance Company
5. Allianz
6. AXA

Chapter 47
Book Publishing

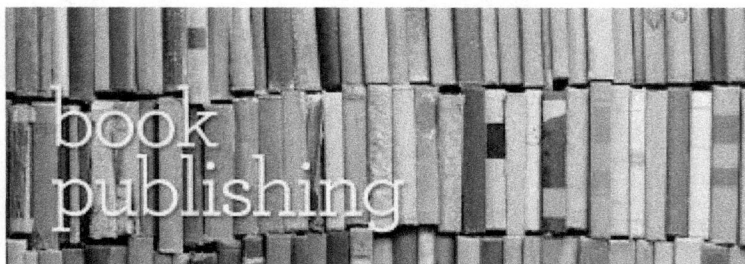

- How are books published?

There are three primary paths to getting books published:

1. Land a traditional publisher who will offer you a book contract. This is "the dream"—what most writers imagine when they think about getting published.

2. Hire a publishing service to help you publish your book. There are many types of publishing services out there, some cheap and some expensive. But the main thing they have in common is that they charge you to publish.

Author Dr Boniface Ikejiani

3. Self-publish. This is where you act as the publisher, and hire the help you need to publish and sell your work, generally through Amazon and other major retailers.

- The cost of publishing a book.

Since the explosion of digital books on Amazon and various other platforms like kobo, ibooks, and smashwords, wanna-be authors and pro authors alike can write, publish and promote their books for less than $1000. On the other hand, you can spend as much as $20,000 on self-publishing and book marketing costs if you have that kind of budget.

- Best publishing companies.

1. Pearson
2. ThomsonReuters
3. RELX Group
4. Wolters Kluwer
5. Penguin Random House
6. Scholaristic
7. Wiley
8. Cengage Learning Holdings II LP
9. Harper Collins
10. Houghton Miffin Harcourt

Author Dr Boniface Ikejiani

Chapter 48
Equipment Manufacture

- What equipment is needed in Nollywood?

In Nollywood and other movie industries, depending on the basis of the budget, there are some mandatory things for the movie production.

Visual Department:

1. Camera
2. Lens
3. Tripod
4. Video Tape/External Memory Card/Hard Drive
5. Reflector

Author Dr Boniface Ikejiani

6. Lighting
7. Laptop
8. Monitor
9. Dolly

Cranes (Rent Charges):

1. Jimmy Jib Crane: 100USD/day
2. Akela Crane: 500USD/day
3. 40 ft crane: 70USD/day

Sound Department:

1. Microphones
a. Shotgun Microphone
b. Handheld Microphones
c. Lapel Microphones
2. Boom Pole + Head Phone
3. Audio Cables + Usual Mic
4. TASCAM DR-600 Mk II

• The best equipment manufacturing companies in Hollywood.

1. Leeper Brothers Inc.
2. Allan Aircraft Supply Co, LLc
3. Ferguson Fire & Fabrication
4. Bobrick Washroom Equipment Inc.

Author Dr Boniface Ikejiani

5. Modern Studio Equipment
6. Applied Industrial Technologies

Author Dr Boniface Ikejiani

Chapter 49
Contract Agreement writing

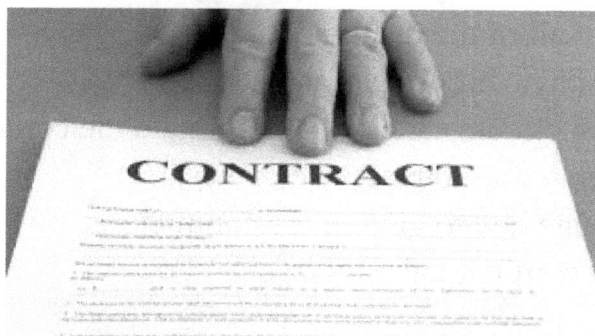

- How to write contract agreement in Nollywood.

There are several sources where you can get standard forms from and adapt for use in your business. If there is a lot of money or important property rights involved, you should have a lawyer do this for you. For most transactions, the attorneys' fees will be too great for you to pay. Remember, some kind of written document is usually preferable to an oral agreement with nothing in writing, even if it is not as comprehensive and well-written as what you might use if you could afford the services of an attorney.

Author Dr Boniface Ikejiani

- Tips for writing the best contract agreement.

1. Get it in writing.
2. Keep it simple.
3. Deal with the right person.
4. Identify each party correctly.
5. Spell out all of the details.
6. Specify payment obligations.
7. Agree on circumstances that terminate the contract.
8. Agree on a way to resolve disputes.
9. Pick a state law to govern the contract.
10. Keep it confidential.

- The importance of writing contract agreement.

Without a written agreement, a judge or jury will have a hard time determining which version of events to believe in a "your word against theirs" scenario.

There are many other reasons to have a written contract besides having evidence to point to during litigation. A written contract ensures that all of the terms of your agreement are documented. If a disagreement arises, there will be a document that the parties can refer back to in order to get the relationship back on track. In short, a solid written contract can save money and strengthen a business relationship by helping to avoid litigation altogether.

Author Dr Boniface Ikejiani

Chapter 50

THE BUSINESS OF NOLLYWOOD

Richard Branson once said,

"You don't learn how to walk by following rules. You learn by doing and falling over."

The film industry in Nigeria knowingly or unknowingly may have adhered to this philosophy as it has evolved outside of the format developed by its predecessors in America, India, China, and Britain to mention a few.

From the street peddling of DHS videocassettes in the early 90s with films like Keneth Nnebue's *Living in Bondage,* which was shot on a budget of $12,000 and sold more than a million copies, Nollywood (as it has been dubbed) sells products globally via cinema, DVDs, television and Internet platforms (*Jake Bright, 2015*).

Author Dr Boniface Ikejiani

To critically analyze the viability of a product, it may be in our interest to identify its end users: the consumers.

According to (*Rebecca Moudio, 2013*), Nollywood was already Nigeria's second largest employer of labor after Agriculture, employing over a million people as at 2013. These people cater to an audience of consumers in every part of the world, mostly, Africans in Africa, Europe, North America and Asia.

(Isabella Akinseye, 2017) claims that by April 2017, Kemi Adetiba's wedding party made a record-breaking box office sales of 450 million naira in Africa alone and was still selling at the time in other parts of the world.

(*Jake Bright, 2015*) further stated that the emergence of new media and online Internet platforms like iROKO (where global subscribers pay $1.50 a month) had attracted financial backing from firms like New York's Tiger Global. This was as much an achievement for the industry as was Nollywood producer, Kunle Afolayan's film, *October 1* added to the already existing 10 Nollywood titles already on Online media content giant; Netflix.

Author Dr Boniface Ikejiani

In 2014, DSTV further granted access to lower income earners when it included the Africa Magic Nollywood movie channels to its GOtv bouquet. This meant that with about $8 a month, Africans could access Nollywood movies and content in about 50 countries in which they operate.

In summary, the consumers are global. This means the market is fertile enough to expand beyond geographical locations.

It should be noted, however, that these movies are done with much lower budgets than their counterparts in Hollywood. But with brands and organizations willing to showcase their ideas, products and generally gain profit from this newfound goldmine, partnerships and sponsorships have begun to improve. The future may be bright for Nollywood after all.

For this analysis on the business of Nollywood, we shall examine the distribution outlets through which the products reach the consumers. These outlets are the same as obtained globally with Hollywood, Bollywood, the Chinese, British and other movie industries. They are:

Author Dr Boniface Ikejiani

1. Cinema
2. Television
3. DVD
4. Online media platforms.

Although this is yet to be exploited in Nollywood, the branding and sales of merchandise from TV contents such as action figures, games, dolls, toys, comic books, books, etc., may be worth the while.

Cinema

We have conducted an interview with a cinema insider to ascertain accurate information on the business of cinema as regards Nollywood.

(*Hannah Graham, 2017*) stated that Cinema movies make between 40million to 200millon naira within a two week to a two-month timeframe. This depends on the quality, advertisement as well as ratings by the viewers and critics.

There are three parties involved in this transaction.

Author Dr Boniface Ikejiani

a. The producer

b. The distributor

c. The exhibitor (Cinema)

The major distribution brands in Nigeria are Silver bird film distribution, film one distribution, blue pictures, homelands and genesis film distribution. There are a few others that are not as influential.

These brands can be reached via information on their websites and social media pages which give numbers, email and physical office addresses which are mostly in the Lagos State of Nigeria.

Amongst all these brands, Silver bird Distribution is the only one currently with a branch outside Nigeria. They also own distribution rights in cinema in Ghana.

Apparently, Silver bird, Genesis, and Film one distribution own their private exhibition outlets or cinemas.

The cinema industry supports independent filmmakers. As an independent producer, one does not really need to belong to any association to get movies exhibited at the cinema.

Author Dr Boniface Ikejiani

Though it is advisable to join the Actor's Guild of Nigeria or the other body called the Association of movie producers, being independent won't hinder the distribution process as long as a producer has a good movie.

The distributors serve as the mediators between the producers and the cinemas who are referred to as the exhibitors.

The distributor shares income from the movies across all the cinemas with the producers at an agreed percentage.

When movies are handed over to exhibitors (cinemas), rights to commercials are exclusively given to the exhibitors.

At best, the producer is given advert slots for another movie of his/hers (most times yet to be released/coming soon).

This is usually done before the main feature movie begins and must be discussed as part of the deal with the distributor.

Exhibitors only interface with the distributor and not with the producer.

Author Dr Boniface Ikejiani

Producers can choose to advertise outside the cinema, which of course goes a long way to help sell the movie.

Adverts and cooperate brandings play very vital roles as people usually have sentimental attachments to brands. In other words, brand endorsements influence patronage of the movie.

However, these brands commercials cannot be advertised in the middle of the show, certainly not with cinema movies. The reason is that the Cinema movies most times run uninterrupted.

Cinemas may also make money by privately advertising brands; hence they hardly allow producers advertise brand commercials during the movie, except there are other charges attached.

This is usually a flexible arrangement based on who is involved. This simply means that a big producer like Steven Spielberg won't be received the same way a first time producer will. He would definitely have the power to demand more.

Author Dr Boniface Ikejiani

However, brand endorsements can be done in the movie trailer/advert. Or even directly within the production process. E.g., Driving an Audi or a BMW in the movie with the logo specially showcased.

The performance of the movie determines how long it will be allowed to stay on the Cinema screen and the corresponding amount it will make at the end of the play.

Some stay from 2 weeks to 2 months or even more. Recently though, screen space is quite limited in most cinemas. With the increasing line-ups and applications to premiere new movies, the exhibitor might just choose to create room for new movies, hence reduce screen time.

Television

Television content business in Nigeria has different ways in which it is marketed. This most times depends on the media house in question. (*Jake Bright, 2015*) showed that the emergence of the South African company, DSTV's GOtv, brought about a boost to the audience number who patronize their Africa magic movie channel. For this reason, the need for good quality content has led to the advent of DSTV buying off content from producers.

According to (*Baseone Oruye, 2017*), these TV stations have a content department who run quality checks on proposed contents from producers before negotiations (if they like and choose to purchase such content).

Producers can access the TV stations directly if they please. This may be via their websites, social media pages or a direct sojourn to their offices in Lagos state of Nigeria.

However, it is wise to note that some stations would redirect producers to *independent content agents*. These can also be found online, but with the need to beware of fraudsters in the Nigerian business clime. It's safer to get referrals from the stations themselves.

These agents usually have the experience of assessing the content beforehand and advising on details like format, file size, medium and expected financial prices per *length of the content* depending on the content.

Author Dr Boniface Ikejiani

The contents could be short films, TV series, full-length movies or documentaries. Whatever the nature of the content, it is mostly priced by the TV stations based on production value and quality. This value may be influenced by the value of the actors/characters involved in the production, the directors/ producer involved, the kind of equipment used, the locations used, the brands affiliated, etc.

The bottom line is that higher quality production fetches higher price tags.

The prevailing prices usually range from about $200 to $700 per TV episode. Movie contents are also valued at around N200, 000 to N500, 000 naira per movie. Higher figures could be given to higher value blockbusters.

The practice of paying producers for content mostly pertains to big players like DSTV, Ebony life TV, Wazobia Max, etc.

It is important to note that most local TV stations in Nigeria take feature-length movie content for free. Meaning that they don't pay producers to show content. The producer is expected to sign a document granting them the right to air the product without any financial obligation. There are times

Author Dr Boniface Ikejiani

that TV stations have showcased content without the consent of the producer. This is typical of smaller local television stations and small-time producers because most low budget producers see this as an avenue to get their names and products out there. Hence, they usually take it.

There is another way in which Nollywood content is aired as well.

This method involves paying the TV station airtime to broadcast the product. This is mostly done with local and national TV stations, as their airtime slots are a lot less expensive in comparison to their multinational counterparts like DSTV, etc.

The seeming advantage that producers have with this option is that they retain complete control over the time slot allocated to them. Thereby, giving them the opportunity to source for as many advert placements within the purchased allocated program duration. The proceeds from these advert slots are solely owned and controlled by the producer in this case.

Author Dr Boniface Ikejiani

DVD

According to (Prince Nwamadi, 2017), the intricacies of DVD marketing of Nollywood products is more complex than it appears. Independent marketers may choose to distribute content from the producer in two ways.

1. By distributing copies of the DVD content mass-produced and handed to them with authorization by the producer. In this process, the producer is paid royalties based on sales made. It should be noted, however, that this process is burdened with the issue of accountability. Distributors have been known to pirate content and give false account to producers who make this deal.

2. The second method is the case where producers sell exclusive distribution rights to the distributor. This is usually restricted to an agreed territory, usually a particular region, a particular country or particular continent. An agreed price is paid in flexible installments to the producer. Sometimes, a one-time full payment may be made. This depends on the personalities involved. This method usually has the producer at the losing end as the marketer usually sells a minimum of 20,000 copies on average. But prices may range from one

Author Dr Boniface Ikejiani

million naira to 5 million naira based on the content, quality, the number of star characters featured, etc. In summary, the DVD marketing process is not very fair to the producer as piracy and marketers take advantage of the producer. Hopefully, this will be tackled someday.

These marketers are found in three major locations in Nigeria. *Alaba international market*, Lagos, *Upper Iweka*, Onitsha and *Pound road*, Aba.

For the safety of the producer, proper physical contact must be made as remote phone conversations have most times ended in scams and other unfortunate eventualities. Sadly, this is a problem with business in Nigeria.

ONLINE MARKETING

According to (Rebecca Moudio, 2013), the emergence of Jason Njoku's iROKOtv created a platform through which Nollywood's contents could be viewed. (Jake Bright, 2015) adds that with as low as $1.50 per month, these contents can be viewed globally by subscribers. Today, Nollywood's content can be found on Netflix, iTunes and other online platforms like YouTube, Facebook, etc.

According to (Zeke, 2014), getting content on Netflix is easier when the producer goes via independent distribution companies. An example of such is Distribber. Distribber charges $1,600 to accept your content, but the producer retains 100% of the revenue the content makes from Netflix and other platforms it distributes to.

After uploading to the Netflix data base, there comes a need for massive publicity. This may require money or ingenuity. Netflix doesn't pay per view; it instead pays the producer a one-time fee for a license (which may last for a year or two) to an unlimited number of viewers.

iTunes can be accessed via a distribution company known as tunecore. They take a percentage form the royalties paid by iTunes.

Irokotv, ibakatv, etc. can be accessed via the information on their sites. As usual with the Nigerian companies, a physical meeting is advised.

Author Dr Boniface Ikejiani

In summary, Nollywood is making gains in terms of improved quality and patronage globally. It has become a gold mine of sorts, providing jobs for millions and gaining revenue for the Nigerian economy. For many, it is great entertainment, but for a few creative's, it is a way for Africans to tell our story, from our perspective.

Cinema listings (United Kingdom)

Cineworld

Empire

Odeon

Showcase

Vue

IMAX

Cinema listings (United States)

Act III Theatres

Alamo drafthouse cinema

American broadcasting paramount

AMC theatres

Author Dr Boniface Ikejiani

Angelika film Centre

Arc light Hollywood

BF Keith circuit

B&B Theatres Bow tie cinemas

Cinecapri

Cineplex Entertainment

Cinemark theatres

Regal entertainment Inc.

Cinepolis

B&B Theatres

Douglas Theatre Company

General cinema Corporation

IMAX Corporation

National Amusements

Premier Cinemas

Showcase Cinemas

United artists Cinemas

United paramount theatres

Author Dr Boniface Ikejiani

Cinema listings (Africa)

Nu Metro Cinemas (South Africa)

Ster-kinekor

Silverbird Cinemas (Nigeria, Ghana)

Film house Cinemas (Nigeria)

Genesis Cinemas (Nigeria)

Online distribution platforms

Netflix

iTunes

YouTube

Irokotv

ibakatv

Author Dr Boniface Ikejiani

References

1. www.wikipedia.com
2. https://www.statista.com/topics/964/film/
3. https://www.theguardian.com/film/film-industry
4. http://historycooperative.org/the-history-of-the-hollywood-movie-industry/
5. http://creativeskillset.org/creative_industries/film/job_roles
6. http://www.newworldencyclopedia.org/entry/Film_industry_(United_States)
7. http://www.vault.com/industriesprofessions/industries/film.aspx
8. http://thegatewayonline.com/commercial-awareness/business-analysis/how-does-the-film-industry-work
9. http://www.angelfire.com/ar2/videomanual1/cam.html
10. https://www.thebalance.com/catering-for-event-planners-1223641
11. http://paintingsinmovies.com
12. http://www.masteringfilm.com/the-role-of-costumes-and-costume-designers/
13. http://learnaboutfilm.com/making-a-film/equipment-for-low-budget-filmmaking/sound-equipment-for-film/
14. https://www.slideshare.net/mobile/shanovitz/lighting-in-film
15. https://www.quora.com/Why-are-soundtracks-important-in-movies
16. http://cosmeticsandskin.com/cdc/early-movie.php
17. http://mentalfloss.com/article/84184/16-behind-scenes-secrets-stunt-performers

Author Dr Boniface Ikejiani

18. Richard Branson (2014), www.virgin.com
19. Isabella   Akinseye   (2017),   Vanguard   Nigeria. www.vanguardngr.com
20. Jake bright (2015) *African Economy, Time Inc.*
21. Rebecca Moudio, Africa Renewal, un.org.
22. Dstv.com
23. Hannah Graham (2017), former Silver bird cinema and film house cinema   manager
24. Prince Nwamadi (2017), Audio/video marketer
25. Baseone Oruye (2017), former head of editing department, Cool TV. Lagos